OXFORD STU

Series Editor: Steven Croft

Alfred, Lord Tennyson

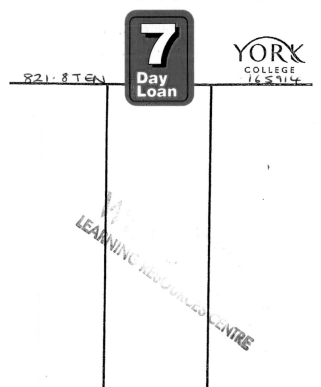

OXFORD
UNIVERSITY PRESS

Great Clarendon Street, Oxford OX2 6DP

Oxford University Press is a department of the University of Oxford.
It furthers the University's objective of excellence in research, scholarship,
and education by publishing worldwide in

Oxford   New York

Auckland   Cape Town   Dar es Salaam   Hong Kong   Karachi
Kuala Lumpur   Madrid   Melbourne   Mexico City   Nairobi
New Delhi   Shanghai   Taipei   Toronto

With offices in

Argentina   Austria   Brazil   Chile   Czech Republic   France   Greece
Guatemala   Hungary   Italy   Japan   South Korea   Poland   Portugal
Singapore   Switzerland   Thailand   Turkey   Ukraine   Vietnam

Oxford is a registered trade mark of Oxford University Press
in the UK and in certain other countries

© Helen Cross 2013

British Library Cataloguing in Publication Data

Data available

ISBN: 978-0-19-912979-9

1 3 5 7 9 10 8 6 4 2

Typeset in India by TNQ Books and Journals Pvt. Ltd.

Printed in China by Printplus

Paper used in the production of this book is a natural, recyclable product made from wood
grown in sustainable forests. The manufacturing process conforms to the environmental
regulations of the country of origin.

The publishers would like to thank the following for permission to reproduce photographs:

Page 6: National Portrait Gallery, London; pages 9, 12 and 14: Mary Evans Picture
Library; page 90: Pellegrini, Carlo (1866–1937)/Private Collection/© Look and
Learn/Peter Jackson Collection/The Bridgeman Art Library; page 104: Collier, John
(1850–1934)/© Herbert Art Gallery & Museum, Coventry, UK/The Bridgeman Art
Library; pages 118 and 123: Getty Images; page 127: Warry (19th century)/
Private Collection/© Look and Learn/The Bridgeman Art Library;
page 133: Time & Life Pictures/Getty Images

Contents

Acknowledgements

The text of the poems is taken from *Alfred Tennyson: The Major Works*, edited by Adam Roberts (Oxford World's Classics, 2000), except *Godiva*, taken from *Tennyson: Poems and Plays*, edited by T. Herbert Warren, revised and enlarged by Frederick Page (Oxford University Press, 1971).

Extracts from the *Authorized Version of the Bible* (*The King James Bible*), the rights in which are vested in the Crown, reproduced by permission of the Crown's Patentee, Cambridge University Press.

Isobel Armstrong: extract from *Victorian Poetry: Poetry, Poetics and Politics* (Routledge, 1993), reprinted by permission of Taylor & Francis Books (UK).

Homer: extract from Book 9, 'In the One-Eyed Giant's Cave', from *The Odyssey* translated by Robert Fagles (Penguin, 1996), translation copyright © Robert Fagles 1996, reprinted by permission of Viking Penguin, a division of Penguin Group (USA) Inc.

Robert Bernard Martin: extracts from *Tennyson: The Unquiet Heart* (Faber, 1980), reprinted by permission of the publishers.

Although we have made every effort to trace and contact copyright holders before publication, this has not been possible in all cases. If notified, the publisher will rectify any errors or omissions at the earliest opportunity.

Acknowledgements from Helen Cross

I am very grateful to Jan Doorly for her unfailing patience and helpfulness as well as her thoughtful editing of this text. I would also like to thank Steven Croft for his useful and encouraging comments, and David Mannion for his support and forbearance.

Editors

Steven Croft, the series editor, holds degrees from Leeds and Sheffield universities. He has taught at secondary and tertiary level and headed the Department of English and Humanities in a tertiary college. He has 25 years' examining experience at A level and is currently a Principal Examiner for English. He has written several books on teaching English at A level, and his publications for Oxford University Press include *Exploring Literature*, *Success in AQA Language and Literature* and *Exploring Language and Literature*.

Helen Cross read English Literature and Music at the University of Glasgow and later was awarded an MA in Life Writing (with distinction) at the University of York. Over the past 20 years she has taught English and English Literature in comprehensive schools and in the private sector. She is an Associate Lecturer for the Open University and has been an examiner in A level English Literature. She has edited *Wilfred Owen: Selected Poems and Letters* and *Literature of the First World War* in this series, and with Steven Croft she is joint author of A level English Literature textbooks published by Oxford University Press including *Exploring Literature* and *Success in Literature*.

Foreword

Oxford Student Texts, under the founding editorship of Victor Lee, have established a reputation for presenting literary texts to students in both a scholarly and an accessible way. The new editions aim to build on this successful approach. They have been written to help students, particularly those studying English literature for AS or A level, to develop an increased understanding of their texts. Each volume in the series, which covers a selection of key poetry and drama texts, consists of four main sections which link together to provide an integrated approach to the study of the text.

The first part provides important background information about the writer, his or her times and the factors that played an important part in shaping the work. This discussion sets the work in context and explores some key contextual factors.

This section is followed by the poetry or play itself. The text is presented without accompanying notes so that students can engage with it on their own terms without the influence of secondary ideas. To encourage this approach, the Notes are placed in the third section, immediately following the text. The Notes provide explanations of particular words, phrases, images, allusions and so forth, to help students gain a full understanding of the text. They also raise questions or highlight particular issues or ideas which are important to consider when arriving at interpretations.

The fourth section, Interpretations, goes on to discuss a range of issues in more detail. This involves an examination of the influence of contextual factors as well as looking at such aspects as language and style, and various critical views or interpretations. A range of activities for students to carry out, together with discussions as to how these might be approached, are integrated into this section.

At the end of each volume there is a selection of Essay Questions, a Chronology, and a Further Reading list.

We hope you enjoy reading this text and working with these supporting materials, and wish you every success in your studies.

Steven Croft   *Series Editor*

Tennyson in Context

What expectations do you bring as you begin studying the work of Alfred, Lord Tennyson? His name alone might seem to place him in another age and at a distance from ordinary life. Many people are familiar with the hypnotic, haunting legend of *The Lady of Shalott* (page 22) and the famous Pre-Raphaelite paintings that illustrate it, while *The Charge of the Light Brigade*, with its rousing military rhythm and celebration of soldierly conduct against all odds (see page 46), is enduringly popular. These are probably the best known, but not necessarily the most typical of his poems.

In fact, it is not easy to identify a typical Tennyson poem, as his work explores an enormous variety of subjects and forms. Along with the common poetic themes of love, loss and death, there are poems that tackle drug addiction (*Choric Song*), ageing (*Tithonus* and *Ulysses*), feminism (*The Princess*), and social change (*Maud*); there are beautiful short lyrics ('*Now sleeps the crimson petal*') and good stories (*Godiva*); and there is a virtuosic use of language which ranges from the bare, heartbreaking expression of grief (*In Memoriam* VII) to the most rich and sumptuous description (*The Lotos-Eaters*).

Poetry in an 'unpoetical' age

For many reasons, the nineteenth century was a time of great change and turmoil. On a global level, the age of empire reached its peak. Russia and Turkey ruled vast territories, and European nations such as Britain, France and Prussia (later Germany) had colonized large areas of the other continents. Napoleon became Emperor of France in 1804 and Prussia evolved to become the German Empire in 1871; the British Empire, which included colonies in India, Australia and New Zealand, the West Indies and Canada, flourished under the rule of Queen Victoria. Inevitably, there was conflict between these 'superpowers', resulting in the Crimean War in 1850s and the Franco-Prussian War in the 1870s.

It was also the era of industrialization. In Britain, at the beginning of the century the economy was still largely rural and agricultural, but by 1850 England had become predominantly urban. With the advent of increasingly sophisticated machinery and mass production, many workers migrated from the countryside to work in factories in the towns and cities; but factory work was depersonalizing and conditions were often poor or even dangerous. In both town and countryside, there was a widening inequality between rich and poor. Inevitably, such a major and rapid transition generated social unrest and contributed to political change. In the 1830s, for example, the 'Tolpuddle Martyrs', six farmworkers from Dorset, were sentenced to transportation to Australia for forming a trade union, but were freed after a campaign of mass demonstrations; in the 1840s the Chartist movement mobilized a large proportion of the population to sign petitions in support of political reform and greater equality.

Old worldviews were being challenged: science and technology were developing rapidly and Charles Darwin's theories of evolution by natural selection posed a major challenge to traditional Christian religious belief. Education became broader, and was also available to far more of the population.

There was a dizzying acceleration in the pace of life. By the 1850s, the railway network was in place and steam trains enabled people to travel much further and faster than they could have imagined 20 years earlier; the instant transmission of messages, through the newly invented telegraph, seemed to defy the limits of time and space. People in the early Victorian era felt that they were living in a 'modern' age and suffered from 'future shock' – the feeling that there was too much change in too short a period of time – no less than those of the twentieth or twenty-first centuries.

Alfred Tennyson lived though most of this turbulent century. Why, then, when we read his work, does it often seem that we are in a very different world? It seems like a personal world, which rarely touches directly on the upheavals going on around him, or an older, more distant world, rooted in tales of the legendary King Arthur or the classical writings of Ancient Greece.

The transformations that affected almost every facet of life in nineteenth-century Britain were reflected in the literary world. In keeping with the new industrial age, the Victorian worldview was coloured by the philosophy of Utilitarianism, which suggested that the value of anything could be measured by its practical usefulness. The 'outer' world of everyday life and work was considered to be the only true and worthwhile 'reality'. By comparison, the 'inner' world of imagination and feeling was dismissed as a useless distraction that made people incapable of giving their full attention to the 'real' aspects of everyday life.

It is not surprising, then, that the literary forms most strongly identified with the Victorian age are those concerned with 'outer reality': the realist novel and non-fiction prose. The great novels of writers such as Charles Dickens and Elizabeth Gaskell engage directly and critically with what was termed the 'condition of England': they address issues such as the impact of industry on human life and the landscape, the inequality of the class system, the struggles of the poor, and the corruption of institutions.

It was an 'unpoetical' time, wrote the poet Matthew Arnold in 1849. So what was happening to poetry?

In earlier centuries, poetry had been more centre-stage in the world of literature and ideas. Tennyson's friend Arthur Hallam wrote that 'In the old times the poetic impulse went along with the general impulse of the nation', but 'the age in which we live comes late in our national progress' and the 'prime' of literature 'is gone, never to return' ('On Some of the Characteristics of Modern Poetry', 1831). During the eighteenth century, poets had been chiefly concerned with voicing thoughts and ideas about the 'outer world'; artificiality was admired and the fashion was for dry, clever, witty language. The Romantic movement that followed was a reaction against this, prioritizing nature and the 'inner'

The life of Alfred Tennyson

What manner of man was this young poet who enthralled all
those who knew him, who was so severe a critic of himself,
who was so doubtful of his powers, and yet who seems to have
felt unshakenly that his business in the world was the making
of great verse? Here is one description of him: 'Six feet high,
broad-chested, strong-limbed, his face Shakespearean, and
with deep eyelids; his forehead ample, crowned with dark
wavy hair, his head finely poised.'... a combination, in fact, of
the athletic young Englishman and of the Greek god.

(Aaron Watson, *Tennyson: A Biography*, page 23)

Alfred Tennyson in a portrait painted in about 1840 by Samuel
Laurence and Sir Edward Burne-Jones

The early part of Tennyson's life was shadowed by family conflict, which had begun before he was born. His father, George Tennyson, was offended because the family home and wealth had passed to his younger brother, Charles. George had been pushed into entering the Church and became rector of the parish of Somersby, a quiet village in Lincolnshire, but he was not suited to the task and found the work uncongenial. Although he was a clever and cultured man, his bitterness and shame, combined with a tendency to depression and mental instability, made him very hard to live with. He often drank too much, was sometimes violent, and eventually became estranged from his wife. Relatively speaking, for the time, the family did not live in real poverty – nowadays we would consider them middle class and quite genteel – but money was always an issue and source of worry. There were 12 children, most of whom shared, to some degree, their father's unstable temperament.

Alfred, the fourth child, was born in 1809. Apart from some years at Louth Grammar School, which he hated so much that in later life he would not go near it, he received most of his education at home, where his father gave him a good grounding in literature, Latin and Greek. He was something of a child prodigy, already thrilled by the power of language and producing poetry at the age of eight or nine, when he announced to his brother that he was 'going to be famous'. Looking back, he wrote:

> When I was in my very earliest teens... I wrote an epic in
> three books. It was full of furious battles... and descriptions
> of lake and mountain scenery which I had never looked upon.
> I never felt so inspired – I used to compose 60 or 70 lines in
> a breath. I used to shout them about the white silent fields,
> leaping over the hedges in my excitement.

In 1827, along with his older brother Charles, he published some of his work for the first time in *Poems by Two Brothers*.

Later, he was to describe this as 'early rot', but it contained some seeds of his later success. In the same year, he became a student at Trinity College, Cambridge, but initially was lonely and dissatisfied, complaining that the teaching was dry and did not 'feed... the heart'.

However, in 1829 he met fellow student Arthur Henry Hallam, and made what was to be the most important friendship of his life. Tennyson was particularly in need of friendship, distressed by events in his family and lacking in confidence. Hallam was supportive and encouraging. Both young men had a tendency to become despondent and they formed a strong bond based on deep mutual understanding and admiration. They were both accepted into the 'Apostles', a secret society of talented Cambridge students; they travelled together in France and Germany, and Hallam became engaged to Tennyson's sister Emily.

Poetry was a passion they shared and Hallam greatly respected Tennyson's talent, seeing him as 'promising fair to be the greatest poet of our generation, perhaps of our century'. He encouraged Tennyson to publish his work and put a lot of energy into promoting his first books, *Poems, Chiefly Lyrical* (1830) and *Poems* (1832). Although Tennyson's family worries were ongoing and his father's death forced him to leave Cambridge without taking his degree, Tennyson enjoyed some happiness at this time. Some reminiscences from *In Memoriam* LXXXIX capture the joy and pleasure he found in his companionship with Hallam, walking or picnicking in the woods, discussing politics and literature, or simply listening to him read:

> O bliss, when all in circle drawn
>   About him, heart and ear were fed
>   To hear him, as he lay and read
> The Tuscan poets on the lawn

Then, in the first week of October 1833, Tennyson received the news that his beloved friend had died suddenly, of a stroke, while on a visit to Vienna.

By all accounts, Hallam was an extraordinarily gifted young man and his death was a terrible shock to all his friends.

The Cambridge circle had for so long regarded him as their centre. With his vivacity, unselfishness and breadth of interests he touched all their lives at so many points that they seemed almost to have lost a part of themselves.

(Sir Charles Tennyson, *Alfred Tennyson*, page 145)

A sketch depicting Tennyson's friend Arthur Hallam

Tennyson suffered such grief that he began to doubt his Christian faith. In a letter to Queen Victoria, written 30 years later, he was to say that Hallam's death had 'seemed to me to shatter all my life so that I desired to die rather than to live'. He published nothing more for 10 years. He had lost not only his friend and prospective brother-in-law, but his foremost supporter and promoter. Although some critics, including John Stuart Mill, had written encouragingly about his work, others, such as J.W. Croker and J.G. Lockhart, had attacked *Poems* (1832) with sarcastic, mocking reviews (see Interpretations page 130). Throughout his life, Tennyson was highly sensitive to such criticism.

He certainly did not stop writing, however. From the depths of his misery and loneliness he produced some of his greatest work. Almost immediately, he began to express his grief in a series of short elegies for his friend. Eventually, over 17 years, these were shaped into his great memorial poem, *In Memoriam A.H.H.*, which explores 'a soul's journey' through the long process of coming to terms with bereavement (see pages 41 and 75). Several other great poems, including *Ulysses* (page 34) and *Tithonus* (page 52) also originate from this time.

During these years, too, he fell in love. First, he developed an unsatisfactory infatuation with Rosa Baring, the daughter of a wealthy neighbour. She was beautiful, but rather superficial and conventional. Her family was also considered too far above his, socially, for him to be a suitable husband. Disappointment with her shallowness, and bitterness at her family's snobbery, added another layer to his sense of disillusionment with life. This episode was one of the seeds of his long narrative poem *Maud* (see pages 48 and 83).

Then, in 1836, he began a much more promising relationship with Emily Sellwood, an old acquaintance who was eventually to become his wife. Things were not straightforward here either. As the writer Thomas Carlyle's wife Jane had remarked when she met Tennyson, there was something about him that must 'capture the heart of women' but 'men of genius never have anything to keep wives upon'. Although they were engaged in 1838, Tennyson could not afford to marry and Emily's father forbade them to write to each other. As well, he sometimes felt unworthy of her and, because of his tendency towards doubt and questioning, she was unsure about his religious beliefs. The impasse was not to be resolved for 12 years.

For much of the 1840s, separated from Emily and plagued by financial difficulties, he struggled with recurrent bouts of depression. His friend Edward FitzGerald, quoted in Christopher Ricks's biography *Tennyson* (see Further Reading page 147), reported that he was at times: 'Really ill, in a nervous way: what with an hereditary tenderness of nerve, and having spoiled what strength he had by incessant smoking &c.'

FitzGerald was an enthusiastic but realistic advocate of Tennyson's work and encouraged him to overcome his self-doubt and publish again.

Poems (1842) was a combination of new works and scrupulously revised versions of the best pieces from his earlier books, representing a variety of subjects and styles. This time, although some reviewers remained unconvinced, his work was highly praised by several famous writers, including Thomas Carlyle, William Thackeray and Charles Dickens. His publisher claimed he had 'made a sensation', and it became the fashion for students at Oxford to read his work aloud to each other. Although this did little to ease his financial problems or his melancholic outlook, his reputation was now established.

Gradually, his situation improved. In 1845, friends succeeded in organizing for him a small royal pension of £200 a year; then, in 1847, he published *The Princess*, a long dramatic poem, partly inspired by the planned opening of Queen's College, the first college in Britain to offer higher education for women. As a whole, this work is now considered rather strange and unsatisfactory, but it does contain some of his finest short lyric poems, including

'*Tears, idle tears*' (see page 40) and '*Now sleeps the crimson petal*' (page 41).

The year 1850 was a real turning point. First, Emily Sellwood was given a draft of *In Memoriam* to read. She was deeply moved and it convinced her that Tennyson shared her Christian faith. They were married in June; *In Memoriam* was published – anonymously, but its authorship was soon recognized – to great acclaim; and by the end of the year, Tennyson had succeeded William Wordsworth as Poet Laureate, a position he was to hold for 42 years, far longer than any poet before or since.

Emily Sellwood (1813–1896) became a devoted wife to Tennyson

From this time onwards, life became increasingly secure and prosperous for Tennyson. Emily was loyal and devoted; not only did she help to establish a more stable, loving family life, but she worked tirelessly as his secretary, organizing appointments and dealing with copious correspondence from enthusiastic readers. They had two sons, the elder named Hallam in honour of his friend. He was soon able to buy a substantial house, Farringford, on the Isle of Wight, chosen partly because it allowed some privacy from the admirers who were beginning to follow him around like the fans of any modern celebrity.

His work was widely read. His poetic 'monodrama' *Maud*, published in 1855 (see pages 48 and 83), which recalled the bitterness of his earlier life with themes of mental instability, snobbery and disappointment in love, was popular although it was considered rather obscure and morbid. With his first set of *Idylls of the King* (1859), which retold stories from the legends of King Arthur, there was no such doubt: 10,000 copies were sold, more than the work of any poet since Byron.

He enjoyed his popularity. He welcomed many visitors to Farringford and took pleasure in reading his work to them. Some rivals even hinted that it had all become *too* comfortable. According to the biographer Aaron Watson, the much younger, much poorer (and presumably envious) poet Francis Thompson wrote:

> visitors tell the same story over and over again: laurels, cedars, fine old house, the grand figure of the Laureate in his blue cloak... amiability, splendid courtesy... smoking-den, pipe, abuses critics; garden, reads 'Guinevere', 'Boadicea', &c.; never-to-be-forgotten visit; visitor goes away hallelujahing and singing of anthems.

Tennyson's comfortable home at Farringford on the Isle of Wight
became a magnet for visitors

In his role as Poet Laureate, Tennyson responded to
national events with poems such as the *Ode on the Death of the
Duke of Wellington* (1852) and *The Charge of the Light Brigade*
(1854, see page 46). He also became acquainted with Queen
Victoria. Her husband, Prince Albert, was a great admirer of
Tennyson's work and when the prince died in 1861, Tennyson
dedicated *Idylls of the King* to his memory. His dedication
ends with these personal and moving words addressed to the
queen:

Break not, O woman's heart, but still endure;
Break not, for thou art Royal, but endure,
Remembering all the beauty of that star
Which shone so close beside Thee that ye made

One light together, but has past and leaves
The Crown a lonely splendour.
                    May all love,
His love, unseen but felt, o'ershadow Thee,
The love of all Thy sons encompass Thee,
The love of all Thy daughters cherish Thee,
The love of all Thy people comfort Thee,
Till God's love set Thee at his side again.

She also found comfort in reading *In Memoriam*. They developed a genuine friendship and corresponded regularly for the remainder of his life. The queen made him a baronet in 1883.

In his later years, he continued to explore a wide range of themes in his poetry, and also wrote a number of plays. He remained a popular and highly regarded figure until his death in 1892. More than any other poet of his time, he had touched the heart of the public. Two quotations cited in Aaron Watson's biography summarize Tennyson's legacy. Watson reports that Lady Anne Ritchie, daughter of Tennyson's friend, the novelist William Thackeray, said:

> It would not be easy for a generation that has grown up to
> the music of Tennyson, that has in a manner beaten time to it
> with the pulse of its life, to imagine what the world would be
> without it.

And Tennyson's son Hallam summed up his father's achievements in these words:

> If I may venture to speak of his special influence over the
> world, my conviction is that its main and enduring factors are
> his power of expression, the perfection of his workmanship,
> his strong common sense, the high purport of his life

and work, his humility, and his open-hearted and helpful sympathy.

(Hallam Tennyson, *Alfred, Lord Tennyson: A Memoir*,
Volume I, page xii)

Tennyson's most striking and significant work dates from the years between 1830 and 1860, and it is from those years that the following selection of highlights has been chosen.

Selected Poems of
Alfred, Lord Tennyson

Mariana

'Mariana in the moated grange'
(Shakespeare, *Measure for Measure*)

With blackest moss the flower-plots
    Were thickly crusted, one and all:
The rusted nails fell from the knots
    That held the pear to the gable-wall.
5 The broken sheds look'd sad and strange:
    Unlifted was the clinking latch;
    Weeded and worn the ancient thatch
Upon the lonely moated grange.
      She only said, 'My life is dreary,
10   He cometh not,' she said;
      She said, 'I am aweary, aweary,
       I would that I were dead!'

Her tears fell with the dews at even;
    Her tears fell ere the dews were dried;
15 She could not look on the sweet heaven,
    Either at morn or eventide.
After the flitting of the bats,
    When thickest dark did trance the sky,
    She drew her casement-curtain by,
20 And glanced athwart the glooming flats.
      She only said, 'The night is dreary,
       He cometh not,' she said;
      She said, 'I am aweary, aweary,
       I would that I were dead!'

25 Upon the middle of the night,
        Waking she heard the night-fowl crow;
    The cock sung out an hour ere light:
        From the dark fen the oxen's low
    Came to her: without hope of change,
30   In sleep she seem'd to walk forlorn,
        Till cold winds woke the gray-eyed morn
    About the lonely moated grange.
            She only said, 'The day is dreary,
                He cometh not,' she said;
35   She said, 'I am aweary, aweary,
                I would that I were dead!'

    About a stone-cast from the wall
        A sluice with blacken'd waters slept,
    And o'er it many, round and small,
40   The cluster'd marish-mosses crept.
    Hard by a poplar shook alway,
        All silver-green with gnarled bark:
        For leagues no other tree did mark
    The level waste, the rounding gray.
45   She only said, 'My life is dreary,
                He cometh not,' she said;
            She said 'I am aweary, aweary
                I would that I were dead!'

    And ever when the moon was low,
50   And the shrill winds were up and away,
    In the white curtain, to and fro,
        She saw the gusty shadow sway.
    But when the moon was very low,
        And wild winds bound within their cell,

55 The shadow of the poplar fell
Upon her bed, across her brow.
  She only said, 'The night is dreary,
   He cometh not,' she said;
  She said 'I am aweary, aweary,
60   I would that I were dead!'

All day within the dreamy house,
 The doors upon their hinges creak'd;
The blue fly sung in the pane; the mouse
 Behind the mouldering wainscot shriek'd,
65 Or from the crevice peer'd about.
  Old faces glimmer'd thro' the doors,
  Old footsteps trod the upper floors,
Old voices called her from without.
  She only said, 'My life is dreary,
70   He cometh not,' she said;
  She said, 'I am aweary, aweary,
   I would that I were dead!'

The sparrow's chirrup on the roof,
 The slow clock ticking, and the sound
75 Which to the wooing wind aloof
 The poplar made, did all confound
Her sense; but most she loathed the hour
  When the thick-moted sunbeam lay
  Athwart the chambers, and the day
80 Was sloping toward his western bower.
  Then said she, 'I am very dreary,
   He will not come,' she said;
  She wept, 'I am aweary, aweary,
   Oh God, that I were dead!'

The Lady of Shalott

Part I

On either side the river lie
Long fields of barley and of rye,
That clothe the wold and meet the sky;
And thro' the field the road runs by
5   To many-tower'd Camelot;
And up and down the people go,
Gazing where the lilies blow
Round an island there below,
     The island of Shalott.

10   Willows whiten, aspens quiver,
Little breezes dusk and shiver
Thro' the wave that runs for ever
By the island in the river
     Flowing down to Camelot.
15   Four gray walls, and four gray towers,
Overlook a space of flowers,
And the silent isle imbowers
     The Lady of Shalott.

By the margin, willow-veil'd,
20   Slide the heavy barges trail'd
By slow horses; and unhail'd
The shallop flitteth silken-sail'd
     Skimming down to Camelot:
But who hath seen her wave her hand?
25   Or at the casement seen her stand?
Or is she known in all the land,
     The Lady of Shalott?

Only reapers, reaping early
In among the bearded barley,
30 Hear a song that echoes cheerly
From the river winding clearly,
    Down to tower'd Camelot:
And by the moon the reaper weary,
Piling sheaves in uplands airy,
35 Listening, whispers ''Tis the fairy
    Lady of Shalott.'

Part II

There she weaves by night and day
A magic web with colours gay.
She has heard a whisper say,
40 A curse is on her if she stay
    To look down to Camelot.
She knows not what the curse may be,
And so she weaveth steadily,
And little other care hath she,
45   The Lady of Shalott.

And moving thro' a mirror clear
That hangs before her all the year,
Shadows of the world appear.
There she sees the highway near
50   Winding down to Camelot:
There the river eddy whirls,
And there the surly village-churls,
And the red cloaks of market girls,
    Pass onward from Shalott.

55 Sometimes a troop of damsels glad,
An abbot on an ambling pad,

Sometimes a curly shepherd-lad,
Or long-hair'd page in crimson clad,
    Goes by to tower'd Camelot;
60 And sometimes thro' the mirror blue
The knights come riding two and two:
She hath no loyal knight and true,
    The Lady of Shalott.

But in her web she still delights
65 To weave the mirror's magic sights,
For often thro' the silent nights
A funeral, with plumes and lights
    And music, went to Camelot:
Or when the moon was overhead,
70 Came two young lovers lately wed;
'I am half sick of shadows,' said
    The Lady of Shalott.

Part III

A bow-shot from her bower-eaves,
He rode between the barley-sheaves,
75 The sun came dazzling thro' the leaves,
And flamed upon the brazen greaves
    Of bold Sir Lancelot.
A red-cross knight for ever kneel'd
To a lady in his shield,
80 That sparkled on the yellow field,
    Beside remote Shalott.

The gemmy bridle glitter'd free,
Like to some branch of stars we see
Hung in the golden Galaxy.
85 The bridle bells rang merrily
    As he rode down to Camelot:

And from his blazon'd baldric slung
A mighty silver bugle hung,
And as he rode his armour rung,
90   Beside remote Shalott.

All in the blue unclouded weather
Thick-jewell'd shone the saddle-leather,
The helmet and the helmet-feather
Burn'd like one burning flame together,
95   As he rode down to Camelot.
As often thro' the purple night,
Below the starry clusters bright,
Some bearded meteor, trailing light,
      Moves over still Shalott.

00 His broad clear brow in sunlight glow'd;
On burnish'd hooves his war-horse trode;
From underneath his helmet flow'd
His coal-black curls as on he rode,
      As he rode down to Camelot.
05 From the bank and from the river
He flash'd into the crystal mirror,
'Tirra lira,' by the river
      Sang Sir Lancelot.

She left the web, she left the loom,
10 She made three paces thro' the room,
She saw the water-lily bloom,
She saw the helmet and the plume,
      She look'd down to Camelot.
Out flew the web and floated wide;
15 The mirror crack'd from side to side;
'The curse is come upon me,' cried
      The Lady of Shalott.

Part IV

In the stormy east-wind straining,
The pale yellow woods were waning,
120   The broad stream in his banks complaining,
Heavily the low sky raining
    Over tower'd Camelot;
Down she came and found a boat
Beneath a willow left afloat,
125   And round about the prow she wrote
    The Lady of Shalott.

And down the river's dim expanse
Like some bold seer in a trance,
Seeing all his own mischance –
130   With a glassy countenance
    Did she look to Camelot.
And at the closing of the day
She loosed the chain, and down she lay;
The broad stream bore her far away,
135   The Lady of Shalott.

Lying, robed in snowy white
That loosely flew to left and right –
The leaves upon her falling light –
Thro' the noises of the night
140   She floated down to Camelot:
And as the boat-head wound along
The willowy hills and fields among,
They heard her singing her last song,
    The Lady of Shalott.

145   Heard a carol, mournful, holy,
Chanted loudly, chanted lowly,

Till her blood was frozen slowly,
And her eyes were darken'd wholly,
    Turn'd to tower'd Camelot.
150 For ere she reach'd upon the tide
The first house by the water-side,
Singing in her song she died,
    The Lady of Shalott.

Under tower and balcony,
155 By garden-wall and gallery,
A gleaming shape she floated by,
Dead-pale between the houses high,
    Silent into Camelot.
Out upon the wharfs they came,
160 Knight and burgher, lord and dame,
And round the prow they read her name,
    The Lady of Shalott.

Who is this? and what is here?
And in the lighted palace near
165 Died the sound of royal cheer;
And they cross'd themselves for fear,
    All the knights at Camelot:
But Lancelot mused a little space;
He said, 'She has a lovely face;
170 God in his mercy lend her grace,
    The Lady of Shalott.'

The Lotos-Eaters

'Courage!' he said, and pointed toward the land,
'This mounting wave will roll us shoreward soon.'
In the afternoon they came unto a land
In which it seemed always afternoon.
5   All round the coast the languid air did swoon,
Breathing like one that hath a weary dream.
Full-faced above the valley stood the moon;
And like a downward smoke, the slender stream
Along the cliff to fall and pause and fall did seem.

10   A land of streams! some, like a downward smoke,
Slow-dropping veils of thinnest lawn, did go;
And some thro' wavering lights and shadows broke,
Rolling a slumbrous sheet of foam below.
They saw the gleaming river seaward flow
15   From the inner land: far off, three mountain-tops,
Three silent pinnacles of aged snow,
Stood sunset-flush'd: and, dew'd with showery drops,
Up-clomb the shadowy pine above the woven copse.

The charmed sunset linger'd low adown
20   In the red West: thro' mountain clefts the dale
Was seen far inland, and the yellow down
Border'd with palm, and many a winding vale
And meadow, set with slender galingale;
A land where all things always seem'd the same!
25   And round about the keel with faces pale,
Dark faces pale against that rosy flame,
The mild-eyed melancholy Lotos-eaters came.

Branches they bore of that enchanted stem,
Laden with flower and fruit, whereof they gave
30   To each, but whoso did receive of them,
And taste, to him the gushing of the wave
Far far away did seem to mourn and rave
On alien shores; and if his fellow spake,
His voice was thin, as voices from the grave;
35   And deep-asleep he seem'd, yet all awake,
And music in his ears his beating heart did make.

They sat them down upon the yellow sand,
Between the sun and moon upon the shore;
And sweet it was to dream of Fatherland,
40   Of child, and wife, and slave; but evermore
Most weary seem'd the sea, weary the oar,
Weary the wandering fields of barren foam.
Then some one said, 'We will return no more;'
And all at once they sang, 'Our island home
45   Is far beyond the wave; we will no longer roam.'

Choric Song

I

There is sweet music here that softer falls
Than petals from blown roses on the grass,
Or night-dews on still waters between walls
Of shadowy granite, in a gleaming pass;
50   Music that gentlier on the spirit lies,
Than tir'd eyelids upon tir'd eyes;
Music that brings sweet sleep down from the blissful skies.
Here are cool mosses deep,

And thro' the moss the ivies creep,
55   And in the stream the long-leaved flowers weep,
And from the craggy ledge the poppy hangs in sleep.

II

Why are we weigh'd upon with heaviness,
And utterly consumed with sharp distress,
While all things else have rest from weariness?
60   All things have rest: why should we toil alone,
We only toil, who are the first of things,
And make perpetual moan,
Still from one sorrow to another thrown:
Nor ever fold our wings,
65   And cease from wanderings,
Nor steep our brows in slumber's holy balm;
Nor harken what the inner spirit sings,
'There is no joy but calm!'
Why should we only toil, the roof and crown of things?

III

70   Lo! in the middle of the wood,
The folded leaf is woo'd from out the bud
With winds upon the branch, and there
Grows green and broad, and takes no care,
Sun-steep'd at noon, and in the moon
75   Nightly dew-fed; and turning yellow
Falls, and floats adown the air.
Lo! sweeten'd with the summer light,
The full-juiced apple, waxing over-mellow,
Drops in a silent autumn night.
80   All its allotted length of days,
The flower ripens in its place,
Ripens and fades, and falls, and hath no toil,
Fast-rooted in the fruitful soil.

IV

Hateful is the dark-blue sky,
85 Vaulted o'er the dark-blue sea.
Death is the end of life; ah, why
Should life all labour be?
Let us alone. Time driveth onward fast,
And in a little while our lips are dumb.
90 Let us alone. What is it that will last?
All things are taken from us, and become
Portions and parcels of the dreadful Past.
Let us alone. What pleasure can we have
To war with evil? Is there any peace
95 In ever climbing up the climbing wave?
All things have rest, and ripen toward the grave
In silence; ripen, fall and cease:
Give us long rest or death, dark death, or dreamful ease.

V

How sweet it were, hearing the downward stream,
100 With half-shut eyes ever to seem
Falling asleep in a half-dream!
To dream and dream, like yonder amber light,
Which will not leave the myrrh-bush on the height;
To hear each other's whisper'd speech;
105 Eating the Lotos day by day,
To watch the crisping ripples on the beach,
And tender curving lines of creamy spray;
To lend our hearts and spirits wholly
To the influence of mild-minded melancholy;
110 To muse and brood and live again in memory,
With those old faces of our infancy
Heap'd over with a mound of grass,
Two handfuls of white dust, shut in an urn of brass!

VI

Dear is the memory of our wedded lives,
115 And dear the last embraces of our wives
And their warm tears: but all hath suffer'd change:
For surely now our household hearths are cold:
Our sons inherit us: our looks are strange:
And we should come like ghosts to trouble joy.
120 Or else the island princes over-bold
Have eat our substance, and the minstrel sings
Before them of the ten years' war in Troy,
And our great deeds, as half-forgotten things.
Is there confusion in the little isle?
125 Let what is broken so remain.
The Gods are hard to reconcile:
'Tis hard to settle order once again.
There *is* confusion worse than death,
Trouble on trouble, pain on pain,
130 Long labour unto aged breath,
Sore task to hearts worn out by many wars
And eyes grown dim with gazing on the pilot-stars.

VII

But, propt on beds of amaranth and moly,
How sweet (while warm airs lull us, blowing lowly)
135 With half-dropt eyelid still,
Beneath a heaven dark and holy,
To watch the long bright river drawing slowly
His waters from the purple hill –
To hear the dewy echoes calling
140 From cave to cave thro' the thick-twined vine –
To watch the emerald-colour'd water falling
Thro' many a wov'n acanthus-wreath divine!
Only to hear and see the far-off sparkling brine,
Only to hear were sweet, stretch'd out beneath the pine.

VIII

145 The Lotos blooms below the barren peak:
The Lotos blows by every winding creek:
All day the wind breathes low with mellower tone:
Thro' every hollow cave and alley lone
Round and round the spicy downs the yellow Lotos-dust
    is blown.
150 We have had enough of action, and of motion we,
Roll'd to starboard, roll'd to larboard, when the surge was
    seething free,
Where the wallowing monster spouted his foam-fountains
    in the sea.
Let us swear an oath, and keep it with an equal mind,
In the hollow Lotos-land to live and lie reclined
155 On the hills like Gods together, careless of mankind.
For they lie beside their nectar, and the bolts are hurl'd
Far below them in the valleys, and the clouds are lightly
    curl'd
Round their golden houses, girdled with the gleaming
    world:
Where they smile in secret, looking over wasted lands,
Blight and famine, plague and earthquake, roaring deeps
160   and fiery sands,
Clanging fights, and flaming towns, and sinking ships, and
    praying hands.
But they smile, they find a music centred in a doleful song
Steaming up, a lamentation and an ancient tale of wrong,
Like a tale of little meaning tho' the words are strong;
165 Chanted from an ill-used race of men that cleave the soil,
Sow the seed, and reap the harvest with enduring toil,
Storing yearly little dues of wheat, and wine and oil;
Till they perish and they suffer – some, 'tis whisper'd –
    down in hell

Suffer endless anguish, others in Elysian valleys dwell,
170 Resting weary limbs at last on beds of asphodel.
Surely, surely, slumber is more sweet than toil, the shore
Than labour in the deep mid-ocean, wind and wave and oar;
Oh rest ye, brother mariners, we will not wander more.

Ulysses

It little profits that an idle king,
By this still hearth, among these barren crags,
Match'd with an aged wife, I mete and dole
Unequal laws unto a savage race,
5 That hoard, and sleep, and feed, and know not me.

I cannot rest from travel: I will drink
Life to the lees: all times I have enjoy'd
Greatly, have suffer'd greatly, both with those
That loved me, and alone; on shore, and when
10 Thro' scudding drifts the rainy Hyades
Vext the dim sea: I am become a name;
For always roaming with a hungry heart
Much have I seen and known; cities of men
And manners, climates, councils, governments,
15 Myself not least, but honour'd of them all;
And drunk delight of battle with my peers,
Far on the ringing plains of windy Troy.
I am a part of all that I have met;
Yet all experience is an arch wherethro'
20 Gleams that untravell'd world whose margin fades
For ever and for ever when I move.
How dull it is to pause, to make an end,
To rust unburnish'd, not to shine in use!

As tho' to breathe were life. Life piled on life
25 Were all too little, and of one to me
Little remains: but every hour is saved
From that eternal silence, something more,
A bringer of new things; and vile it were
For some three suns to store and hoard myself,
30 And this gray spirit yearning in desire
To follow knowledge like a sinking star,
Beyond the utmost bound of human thought.

This is my son, mine own Telemachus,
To whom I leave the sceptre and the isle –
35 Well-loved of me, discerning to fulfil
This labour, by slow prudence to make mild
A rugged people, and thro' soft degrees
Subdue them to the useful and the good.
Most blameless is he, centred in the sphere
40 Of common duties, decent not to fail
In offices of tenderness, and pay
Meet adoration to my household gods,
When I am gone. He works his work, I mine.

There lies the port; the vessel puffs her sail:
45 There gloom the dark, broad seas. My mariners,
Souls that have toil'd, and wrought, and thought with me –
That ever with a frolic welcome took
The thunder and the sunshine, and opposed
Free hearts, free foreheads – you and I are old;
50 Old age hath yet his honour and his toil;
Death closes all: but something ere the end,
Some work of noble note, may yet be done,
Not unbecoming men that strove with Gods.
The lights begin to twinkle from the rocks:
55 The long day wanes: the slow moon climbs: the deep

Moans round with many voices. Come, my friends,
'Tis not too late to seek a newer world.
Push off, and sitting well in order smite
The sounding furrows; for my purpose holds
60 To sail beyond the sunset, and the baths
Of all the western stars, until I die.
It may be that the gulfs will wash us down:
It may be we shall touch the Happy Isles,
And see the great Achilles, whom we knew.
65 Tho' much is taken, much abides; and tho'
We are not now that strength which in old days
Moved earth and heaven; that which we are, we are;
One equal temper of heroic hearts,
Made weak by time and fate, but strong in will
70 To strive, to seek, to find, and not to yield.

Godiva

I waited for the train at Coventry;
I hung with grooms and porters on the bridge,
To watch the three tall spires; and there I shaped
The city's ancient legend into this:–

5   Not only we, the latest seed of Time,
New men, that in the flying of a wheel
Cry down the past, not only we, that prate
Of rights and wrongs, have loved the people well,
And loathed to see them overtax'd; but she
10 Did more, and underwent, and overcame,
The woman of a thousand summers back,
Godiva, wife to that grim Earl, who ruled
In Coventry: for when he laid a tax

Upon his town, and all the mothers brought
15 Their children, clamouring, 'If we pay, we starve!'
She sought her lord, and found him, where he strode
About the hall, among his dogs, alone,
His beard a foot before him and his hair
A yard behind. She told him of their tears,
20 And pray'd him, 'If they pay this tax, they starve.'
Whereat he stared, replying, half-amazed,
'You would not let your little finger ache
For such as *these*?' – 'But I would die,' said she.
He laugh'd, and swore by Peter and by Paul:
25 Then fillip'd at the diamond in her ear;
'Oh ay, ay, ay, you talk!' – 'Alas!' she said,
'But prove me what it is I would not do.'
And from a heart as rough as Esau's hand,
He answer'd, 'Ride you naked thro' the town,
30 And I repeal it;' and nodding, as in scorn,
He parted, with great strides among his dogs.

So left alone, the passions of her mind,
As winds from all the compass shift and blow,
Made war upon each other for an hour,
35 Till pity won. She sent a herald forth,
And bade him cry, with sound of trumpet, all
The hard condition; but that she would loose
The people: therefore, as they loved her well,
From then till noon no foot should pace the street,
40 No eye look down, she passing; but that all
Should keep within, door shut, and window barr'd.

Then fled she to her inmost bower, and there
Unclasp'd the wedded eagles of her belt,
The grim Earl's gift; but ever at a breath
45 She linger'd, looking like a summer moon

Half-dipt in cloud: anon she shook her head,
And shower'd the rippled ringlets to her knee;
Unclad herself in haste; adown the stair
Stole on; and, like a creeping sunbeam, slid
50   From pillar unto pillar, until she reach'd
The gateway; there she found her palfrey trapt
In purple blazon'd with armorial gold.

Then she rode forth, clothed on with chastity:
The deep air listen'd round her as she rode,
55   And all the low wind hardly breathed for fear.
The little wide-mouth'd heads upon the spout
Had cunning eyes to see: the barking cur
Made her cheek flame: her palfrey's foot-fall shot
Light horrors thro' her pulses: the blind walls
60   Were full of chinks and holes; and overhead
Fantastic gables, crowding, stared: but she
Not less thro' all bore up, till, last, she saw
The white-flower'd elder-thicket from the field
Gleam thro' the Gothic archway in the wall.

65   Then she rode back, clothed on with chastity
And one low churl, compact of thankless earth,
The fatal byword of all years to come,
Boring a little auger-hole in fear,
Peep'd – but his eyes, before they had their will,
70   Were shrivell'd into darkness in his head,
And dropt before him. So the Powers, who wait
On noble deeds, cancell'd a sense misused;
And she, that knew not, pass'd: and all at once,
With twelve great shocks of sound, the shameless noon
75   Was clash'd and hammer'd from a hundred towers,
One after one: but even then she gain'd

Her bower; whence reissuing, robed and crown'd,
To meet her lord, she took the tax away
And built herself an everlasting name.

'Break, break, break'

Break, break, break,
    On thy cold gray stones, O Sea!
And I would that my tongue could utter
    The thoughts that arise in me.

5 O well for the fisherman's boy,
    That he shouts with his sister at play!
O well for the sailor lad,
    That he sings in his boat on the bay!

And the stately ships go on
10   To their haven under the hill;
But O for the touch of a vanish'd hand,
    And the sound of a voice that is still!

Break, break, break
    At the foot of thy crags, O Sea!
15 But the tender grace of a day that is dead
    Will never come back to me.

'Tears, idle tears' (from
The Princess)

Tears, idle tears, I know not what they mean,
Tears from the depth of some divine despair
Rise in the heart, and gather to the eyes,
In looking on the happy Autumn-fields,
5   And thinking of the days that are no more.

Fresh as the first beam glittering on a sail,
That brings our friends up from the underworld,
Sad as the last which reddens over one
That sinks with all we love below the verge;
10   So sad, so fresh, the days that are no more.

Ah, sad and strange as in dark summer dawns
The earliest pipe of half-awaken'd birds
To dying ears, when unto dying eyes
The casement slowly grows a glimmering square;
15   So sad, so strange, the days that are no more.

Dear as remember'd kisses after death,
And sweet as those by hopeless fancy feign'd
On lips that are for others; deep as love,
Deep as first love, and wild with all regret;
20   O Death in Life, the days that are no more.

'Now sleeps the crimson petal'
(from *The Princess*)

Now sleeps the crimson petal, now the white;
Nor waves the cypress in the palace walk;
Nor winks the gold fin in the porphyry font:
The fire-fly wakens: waken thou with me.

5   Now droops the milkwhite peacock like a ghost,
And like a ghost she glimmers on to me.

Now lies the Earth all Danaë to the stars,
And all thy heart lies open unto me.

Now slides the silent meteor on, and leaves
10   A shining furrow, as thy thoughts in me.

Now folds the lily all her sweetness up,
And slips into the bosom of the lake:
So fold thyself, my dearest, thou, and slip
Into my bosom and be lost in me.

In Memoriam A.H.H.

V

I sometimes hold it half a sin
    To put in words the grief I feel;
    For words, like Nature, half reveal
And half conceal the Soul within.

5   But, for the unquiet heart and brain,
        A use in measured language lies;
        The sad mechanic exercise,
Like dull narcotics, numbing pain.

In words, like weeds, I'll wrap me o'er,
10   Like coarsest clothes against the cold:
        But that large grief which these enfold
Is given in outline and no more.

VII

Dark house, by which once more I stand
        Here in the long unlovely street,
        Doors, where my heart was used to beat
So quickly, waiting for a hand,

5   A hand that can be clasp'd no more –
        Behold me, for I cannot sleep,
        And like a guilty thing I creep
At earliest morning to the door.

He is not here; but far away
10   The noise of life begins again,
        And ghastly thro' the drizzling rain
On the bald street breaks the blank day.

XXIV

And was the day of my delight
        As pure and perfect as I say?
        The very source and fount of Day
Is dash'd with wandering isles of night.

5   If all was good and fair we met,
        This earth had been the Paradise

It never look'd to human eyes
Since our first Sun arose and set.

And is it that the haze of grief
10   Makes former gladness loom so great?
      The lowness of the present state,
That sets the past in this relief?

Or that the past will always win
      A glory from its being far;
15   And orb into the perfect star
We saw not, when we moved therein?

L

Be near me when my light is low,
      When the blood creeps, and the nerves prick
      And tingle; and the heart is sick,
And all the wheels of Being slow.

5 Be near me when the sensuous frame
      Is rack'd with pangs that conquer trust;
      And Time, a maniac scattering dust,
And Life, a Fury slinging flame.

Be near me when my faith is dry,
10   And men the flies of latter spring,
      That lay their eggs, and sting and sing
And weave their petty cells and die.

Be near me when I fade away,
      To point the term of human strife,
15   And on the low dark verge of life
The twilight of eternal day.

LXVII

When on my bed the moonlight falls,
    I know that in thy place of rest
    By that broad water of the west,
There comes a glory on the walls;

5   Thy marble bright in dark appears,
    As slowly steals a silver flame
    Along the letters of thy name,
And o'er the number of thy years.

The mystic glory swims away;
10   From off my bed the moonlight dies;
    And closing eaves of wearied eyes
I sleep till dusk is dipt in gray:

And then I know the mist is drawn
    A lucid veil from coast to coast,
15   And in the dark church like a ghost
Thy tablet glimmers to the dawn.

CVI

Ring out, wild bells, to the wild sky,
    The flying cloud, the frosty light:
    The year is dying in the night;
Ring out, wild bells, and let him die.

5   Ring out the old, ring in the new,
    Ring, happy bells, across the snow:
    The year is going, let him go;
Ring out the false, ring in the true.

Ring out the grief that saps the mind,
10   For those that here we see no more;

Ring out the feud of rich and poor,
Ring in redress to all mankind.

Ring out a slowly dying cause,
And ancient forms of party strife;
15   Ring in the nobler modes of life,
With sweeter manners, purer laws.

Ring out the want, the care, the sin,
The faithless coldness of the times;
Ring out, ring out my mournful rhymes,
20   But ring the fuller minstrel in.

Ring out false pride in place and blood,
The civic slander and the spite;
Ring in the love of truth and right,
Ring in the common love of good.

25   Ring out old shapes of foul disease;
Ring out the narrowing lust of gold;
Ring out the thousand wars of old,
Ring in the thousand years of peace.

Ring in the valiant man and free,
30   The larger heart, the kindlier hand;
Ring out the darkness of the land,
Ring in the Christ that is to be.

CXV

Now fades the last long streak of snow,
Now burgeons every maze of quick
About the flowering squares, and thick
By ashen roots the violets blow.

5   Now rings the woodland loud and long,
        The distance takes a lovelier hue,
        And drown'd in yonder living blue
    The lark becomes a sightless song.

    Now dance the lights on lawn and lea,
10   The flocks are whiter down the vale,
        And milkier every milky sail
    On winding stream or distant sea;

    Where now the seamew pipes, or dives
        In yonder greening gleam, and fly
15   The happy birds, that change their sky
    To build and brood; that live their lives

    From land to land; and in my breast
        Spring wakens too; and my regret
        Becomes an April violet,
20   And buds and blossoms like the rest.

The Charge of the Light Brigade

I

Half a league, half a league,
    Half a league onward,
All in the valley of Death
    Rode the six hundred.
5   'Forward, the Light Brigade!
Charge for the guns!' he said:
Into the valley of Death
    Rode the six hundred.

II

'Forward, the Light Brigade!'
10   Was there a man dismay'd?
Not tho' the soldier knew
      Some one had blunder'd:
Their's not to make reply,
Their's not to reason why,
15   Their's but to do and die:
Into the valley of Death
      Rode the six hundred.

III

Cannon to right of them,
Cannon to left of them,
20   Cannon in front of them
      Volley'd and thunder'd;
Storm'd at with shot and shell,
Boldly they rode and well,
Into the jaws of Death,
25   Into the mouth of Hell
      Rode the six hundred.

IV

Flash'd all their sabres bare,
Flash'd as they turn'd in air
Sabring the gunners there,
30   Charging an army, while
      All the world wonder'd:
Plunged in the battery-smoke
Right thro' the line they broke;
Cossack and Russian
35   Reel'd from the sabre-stroke
      Shatter'd and sunder'd.

47

Then they rode back, but not
   Not the six hundred.

V

Cannon to right of them,
40   Cannon to left of them,
Cannon behind them
   Volley'd and thunder'd;
Storm'd at with shot and shell,
While horse and hero fell,
45   They that had fought so well
Came thro' the jaws of Death
Back from the mouth of Hell,
All that was left of them,
   Left of six hundred.

VI

50   When can their glory fade?
O the wild charge they made!
   All the world wonder'd.
Honour the charge they made!
Honour the Light Brigade,
55   Noble six hundred!

Maud

Part II

IV

O that 'twere possible
After long grief and pain

To find the arms of my true love
Round me once again!

5 When I was wont to meet her
In the silent woody places
By the home that gave me birth,
We stood tranced in long embraces
Mixt with kisses sweeter sweeter
10 Than anything on earth.

A shadow flits before me,
Not thou, but like to thee:
Ah Christ, that it were possible
For one short hour to see
15 The souls we loved, that they might tell us
What and where they be.

It leads me forth at evening,
It lightly winds and steals
In a cold white robe before me,
20 When all my spirit reels
At the shouts, the leagues of lights,
And the roaring of the wheels.

Half the night I waste in sighs,
Half in dreams I sorrow after
25 The delight of early skies;
In a wakeful doze I sorrow
For the hand, the lips, the eyes,
For the meeting of the morrow,
The delight of happy laughter,
30 The delight of low replies.

'Tis a morning pure and sweet,
And a dewy splendour falls

49

On the little flower that clings
To the turrets and the walls;
35   'Tis a morning pure and sweet,
And the light and shadow fleet;
She is walking in the meadow,
And the woodland echo rings;
In a moment we shall meet;
40   She is singing in the meadow
And the rivulet at her feet
Ripples on in light and shadow
To the ballad that she sings.

Do I hear her sing as of old,
45   My bird with the shining head,
My own dove with the tender eye?
But there rings on a sudden a passionate cry,
There is some one dying or dead,
And a sullen thunder is roll'd;
50   For a tumult shakes the city,
And I wake, my dream is fled;
In the shuddering dawn, behold,
Without knowledge, without pity,
By the curtains of my bed
55   That abiding phantom cold.

Get thee hence, nor come again,
Mix not memory with doubt,
Pass, thou deathlike type of pain,
Pass and cease to move about!
60   'Tis the blot upon the brain
That *will* show itself without.

Then I rise, the eavedrops fall,
And the yellow vapours choke

The great city sounding wide;
65   The day comes, a dull red ball
Wrapt in drifts of lurid smoke
On the misty river-tide.

Thro' the hubbub of the market
I steal, a wasted frame,
70   It crosses here, it crosses there,
Thro' all that crowd confused and loud,
The shadow still the same;
And on my heavy eyelids
My anguish hangs like shame.

75   Alas for her that met me,
That heard me softly call,
Came glimmering thro' the laurels
At the quiet evenfall,
In the garden by the turrets
80   Of the old manorial hall.

Would the happy spirit descend,
From the realms of light and song,
In the chamber or the street,
As she looks among the blest,
85   Should I fear to greet my friend
Or to say 'Forgive the wrong,'
Or to ask her, 'Take me, sweet,
To the regions of thy rest'?

But the broad light glares and beats,
90   And the shadow flits and fleets
And will not let me be;
And I loathe the squares and streets,
And the faces that one meets,

Hearts with no love for me:
95   Always I long to creep
Into some still cavern deep,
There to weep, and weep, and weep
My whole soul out to thee.

V

Dead, long dead,
Long dead!
And my heart is a handful of dust,
And the wheels go over my head,
5   And my bones are shaken with pain,
For into a shallow grave they are thrust,
Only a yard beneath the street,
And the hoofs of the horses beat, beat,
The hoofs of the horses beat,
10 Beat into my scalp and my brain,
With never an end to the stream of passing feet,
Driving, hurrying, marrying, burying,
Clamour and rumble, and ringing and clatter,
And here beneath it is all as bad,
15 For I thought the dead had peace, but it is not so;
To have no peace in the grave, is that not sad?
But up and down and to and fro,
Ever about me the dead men go;
And then to hear a dead man chatter
20 Is enough to drive one mad.

Tithonus

The woods decay, the woods decay and fall,
The vapours weep their burthen to the ground,
Man comes and tills the field and lies beneath,

And after many a summer dies the swan.
5   Me only cruel immortality
Consumes: I wither slowly in thine arms,
Here at the quiet limit of the world,
A white-hair'd shadow roaming like a dream
The ever-silent spaces of the East,
10 Far-folded mists, and gleaming halls of morn.

     Alas! for this gray shadow, once a man –
So glorious in his beauty and thy choice,
Who madest him thy chosen, that he seem'd
To his great heart none other than a God!
15 I ask'd thee, 'Give me immortality.'
Then didst thou grant mine asking with a smile,
Like wealthy men who care not how they give.
But thy strong Hours indignant work'd their wills,
And beat me down and marr'd and wasted me,
20 And tho' they could not end me, left me maim'd
To dwell in presence of immortal youth,
Immortal age beside immortal youth,
And all I was, in ashes. Can thy love,
Thy beauty, make amends, tho' even now,
25 Close over us, the silver star, thy guide,
Shines in those tremulous eyes that fill with tears
To hear me? Let me go: take back thy gift:
Why should a man desire in any way
To vary from the kindly race of men,
30 Or pass beyond the goal of ordinance
Where all should pause, as is most meet for all?

     A soft air fans the cloud apart; there comes
A glimpse of that dark world where I was born.
Once more the old mysterious glimmer steals
35 From thy pure brows, and from thy shoulders pure,

53

And bosom beating with a heart renew'd.
Thy cheek begins to redden thro' the gloom,
Thy sweet eyes brighten slowly close to mine,
Ere yet they blind the stars, and the wild team
40 Which love thee, yearning for thy yoke, arise,
And shake the darkness from their loosen'd manes,
And beat the twilight into flakes of fire.

Lo! ever thus thou growest beautiful
In silence, then before thine answer given
45 Departest, and thy tears are on my cheek.

Why wilt thou ever scare me with thy tears,
And make me tremble lest a saying learnt,
In days far-off, on that dark earth, be true?
'The Gods themselves cannot recall their gifts.'

50 Ay me! ay me! with what another heart
In days far-off, and with what other eyes
I used to watch – if I be he that watch'd –
The lucid outline forming round thee; saw
The dim curls kindle into sunny rings;
55 Changed with thy mystic change, and felt my blood
Glow with the glow that slowly crimson'd all
Thy presence and thy portals, while I lay,
Mouth, forehead, eyelids, growing dewy-warm
With kisses balmier than half-opening buds
60 Of April, and could hear the lips that kiss'd
Whispering I knew not what of wild and sweet,
Like that strange song I heard Apollo sing,
While Ilion like a mist rose into towers.

Yet hold me not for ever in thine East:
65 How can my nature longer mix with thine?

Coldly thy rosy shadows bathe me, cold
Are all thy lights, and cold my wrinkled feet
Upon thy glimmering thresholds, when the steam
Floats up from those dim fields about the homes
70 Of happy men that have the power to die,
And grassy barrows of the happier dead.
Release me, and restore me to the ground;
Thou seest all things, thou wilt see my grave:
Thou wilt renew thy beauty morn by morn;
75 I earth in earth forget these empty courts,
And thee returning on thy silver wheels.

Crossing the Bar

Sunset and evening star,
    And one clear call for me!
And may there be no moaning of the bar,
    When I put out to sea,

5 But such a tide as moving seems asleep,
    Too full for sound and foam,
When that which drew from out the boundless deep
    Turns again home.

Twilight and evening bell,
10   And after that the dark!
And may there be no sadness of farewell,
    When I embark;

For tho' from out our bourne of Time and Place
    The flood may bear me far,
15 I hope to see my Pilot face to face
    When I have crost the bar.

Notes

Mariana

Tennyson based this poem loosely on a situation from Shakespeare's dark comedy *Measure for Measure*. Mariana, a young gentlewoman, has been abandoned by her fiancé, Angelo (a severe, judgemental magistrate), because her marriage dowry has been lost in a shipwreck in which her brother died. In Act III Scene I we learn that 'this well-seeming Angelo... Left her in her tears, and dried not one of them with his comfort'; although his 'unjust unkindness... in all reason should have quenched her love', it has only increased it.

She has taken refuge in an isolated 'moated grange', an old fortified house attached to a monastery, and waits, miserable and 'dejected', for him to change his mind. Her friends consider it would be better if death could 'take this poor maid from the world'. But after various deceptions and changes of identity, the situation is resolved: Angelo is taught a lesson – judge not, that ye be not judged – and the couple are eventually married.

Tennyson's poem does not engage with this story as a narrative or bring it to any resolution. There is no action, only an evocation of Mariana's *dreary* (9) state of mind as she waits *without hope of change* (29) in the *moated grange*. It is as if time is frozen or suspended; even Mariana herself does not really materialize as a person. We hear her voice repeatedly intoning her refrain, but mainly the poem works through its presentation of her surroundings and the detailed description of what she sees and hears.

Each stanza consists of eight lines of description, either of the landscape or of Mariana herself, with a regular pattern of rhyme and rhythm, followed by a repeated refrain spoken by Mariana.

Isobel Armstrong, in *Victorian Poetry* (see Interpretations pages 134–5), points out that the poem also echoes *Wilhelm Meister's Apprenticeship* (1796), a novel by the German Romantic writer

Johann Wolfgang von Goethe, where a character named Mariana is also abandoned by her lover. Goethe's Mariana is very different from Shakespeare's character. She is an actress and courtesan, and is pregnant with Wilhelm's child when he deserts her; before dying in childbirth, she writes letters to him which are paralleled in Tennyson's refrain.

First published in 1830, Tennyson's poem was included in later collections in 1842 and then in 1870, when it was categorized as juvenilia. Tennyson commented: 'The *moated grange* was no particular grange, but one which rose to the music of Shakespeare's words.'

1–8   What mood is created in this opening stanza? Look carefully at the choice of vocabulary and at the way sound effects are used in these lines. You will notice several examples of alliteration, assonance and internal rhyme. How do these contribute to the description of decay and dishevelment here?

4   **pear**   In earlier editions, this was a 'peach'; Tennyson made the alteration in 1860, as he felt 'peach' did not fit the desolate scene, which was based on the bleak, exceptionally flat landscape of the Lincolnshire fens.

9–12   This refrain recurs, with minor variations, in each of the seven stanzas. What is the effect of this insistent repetition?

18   **trance**   charm, entrance, or put into a trance. The night sky seems unnaturally still.

20   **athwart**   across.
      flats   mud-flats or flat fields.

28   **fen**   marsh or drained marshland.

31   **gray-eyed morn**   This is a quotation from Shakespeare, *Romeo and Juliet* Act II Scene III.

37   **stone-cast**   stone's throw.

38   **sluice**   small pool.

40   **marish**   marsh.

41   **poplar**   It is sometimes suggested that the single tall poplar tree in the flat, empty landscape echoes Mariana's obsession with her lover and is a phallic symbol, or representation of his masculinity.

43 **leagues**   A league was roughly the distance a person could walk in an hour, or around three miles.
54 **cell**   In Greek mythology, Aeolus kept the stormy winds locked in a cell, but if the gods commanded it, he would release them to cause devastating storms.
64 **wainscot**   wooden panelling.
76 **confound**   confuse, perplex.
78 **thick-moted**   full of specks of dust (which catch the light).
80 **sloping toward his western bower**   i.e. the sun was beginning to set.
82–4   What is the effect of the alterations in this final refrain?

The Lady of Shalott

Like *Mariana*, *The Lady of Shalott* is a tale of a woman isolated from the world and destroyed by love, but this poem is more active and dramatic. As a boy, Tennyson developed an interest in Arthurian legends: the world of Camelot, King Arthur and the Knights of the Round Table. He returned to this many times in his life as a source of ideas and material for poetry.

This famous poem is based on the Arthurian tale of Lancelot and Elaine, or Elaine of Astolat. Tennyson said he had taken the story from a version in an Italian novelette, *La Donna di Scalotta*, written early in the fourteenth century, and that he had changed the name because he preferred the 'softer sound' of 'Shalott'. However, the model is not followed closely.

Part I introduces the mystery of the *Lady* who lives in a castle on an island in the river that flows *down to Camelot*. The setting is a rural landscape of *Long fields* and *wolds*, reminiscent of Tennyson's native Lincolnshire. Barges travel up and down the river and many people pass by on the road. They seem to know of the lady's existence but have no contact with her.

Part II explains that she is the victim of a strange curse. She is compelled to spend her time weaving pictures of life in the outside world, but she is only allowed to view this as reflections in a mirror; she must not break this rule and look directly out at the world, or she will die. Although she *still delights* in the *magic sights* in her mirror, she has become weary of seeing only *shadows* of the world.

Part III describes *bold Sir Lancelot* riding by, handsome, brilliant and full of life. Seeing him, in all his glory, reflected in her mirror is too much for her. She leaves her loom, looks through the window and is immediately overcome by the curse.

Part IV relates the outcome of the curse. The weather has become *stormy*, reflecting the change of mood. The lady comes out of her tower, unties a boat, lies down in it and floats down to Camelot, singing her *last song* in a *mournful* voice until she dies. The knights and townspeople of Camelot find her and are fearful. Lancelot, oblivious of his own role in the drama, ironically comments on her *lovely face*.

The poem was first published in 1832, but revised for inclusion in *Poems* (1842). Tennyson's son Hallam reports that it was criticized for being a 'tale of magic symbolism' rather than an allegory with a clear meaning or message; the critic William Jerdan, writing in the *Literary Gazette* in 1832, called it 'a strange ballad without a perceptible object' and even more bitingly referred to it as 'Tennyson's Shalott, an onion which could make nobody shed tears'. (A shallot is a type of small onion.) However, this atmospheric poem has held a fascination for many people. It also inspired several famous paintings by members of the Pre-Raphaelite movement, such as William Holman Hunt and John Everett Millais in the 1850s, and later, by John William Waterhouse (see Interpretations page 118).

3 **wold**   low hills interspersed with steep valleys. This is a
geographical feature typical of Tennyson's native Lincolnshire;
the soil is clay or chalk.

5 **many-tower'd Camelot**   the legendary British city and castle
where King Arthur held his court, and the setting for tales
of the Knights of the Round Table. Its location is unknown.
Several towns in England and Wales have claimed to be
Camelot, for tourist purposes.

10 **Willows whiten** The underside of willow leaves is pale, so
when the wind exposes them the colour of the tree appears to
whiten.

22 **shallop** light boat, fitted with sails, oars, or both. Notice the
effect of sibilance in this line.

52 **churls** countrymen or peasants.

56 **ambling pad** slow-moving horse.

62 **no loyal knight and true** In the world of chivalry, a lady
would be attended by a knight who would honour, protect
and serve her; stating that she has no knight to attend her
emphasizes the isolation and loneliness of the Lady of
Shalott.

69–72 Hallam Tennyson, in his *Memoir*, suggests that the 'key to this
tale' is to be found in these lines, which have 'deep human
significance'.

73–108 What is the effect of the description of Sir Lancelot, in
comparison with the mood in parts I and II? Consider
vocabulary, imagery and use of colour.

76 **brazen greaves** brass leg-armour.

78–9 The Redcross Knight is the hero of Book I of Edmund
Spenser's epic allegorical poem *The Faerie Queene*
(1590–96). He overcomes a dragon, in the service of a
young woman. He is also identified with St George, patron
saint of England and associated with courage and justice.
Lancelot's shield carries a painting of the knight kneeling
to his lady.

82 **gemmy** covered in jewels.

83 **branch of stars** constellation.

87 **blazon'd** decorated with a coat of arms.
baldric belt worn across the chest, from which a shield could
be hung.

107 **'Tirra lira'** These words imitate musical sounds.

128 **seer** clairvoyant; someone who can see into the future.

129 **mischance** bad luck.

130 **glassy countenance** expressionless face.

160 **burgher** middle-class citizen.

166 **cross'd themselves** Christians make the sign of
the cross as a blessing or to invoke God's protection
from evil.

The Lotos-Eaters and Choric Song

In the classical epic poem the *Odyssey*, the ancient Greek poet Homer recounts the mythical story of the hero Ulysses, and the many adventures and challenges he and his mariners must overcome on their eventful voyage home after the Trojan War. (For more on this, see also the headnote to *Ulysses*, page 66.) Tennyson bases his poem on an incident in Book 9 of the *Odyssey*: they arrive at the land of the Lotus-eaters, where the inhabitants eat nothing but the *enchanted… flower and fruit* (28–9) of the lotus plant, a drug with a narcotic effect. Those who take it sink into a drowsy state of self-absorbed idleness, in which they lose all awareness of others and all motivation for action. Ulysses sends some of his men to investigate:

> and soon enough
> they mingled among the natives, Lotus-eaters, Lotus-eaters
> who had no notion of killing my companions, not at all,
> they simply gave them the lotus to taste instead…
> Any crewmen who ate the lotus, the honey-sweet fruit,
> lost all desire to send a message back, much less return,
> their only wish to linger there with the Lotus-eaters,
> grazing on lotus, all memory of the journey home
> dissolved forever.
> (*Odyssey*, Book 9, lines 102–110, translated by Robert Fagles)

Eventually Ulysses has to drag the men, weeping, back to the ship, tie them to their rowing benches and force them to continue with the voyage.

Tennyson's version is in two parts. First, *The Lotos-Eaters* sets the scene and narrates how the men succumb to the *Lotos-eaters*. These five 'Spenserian' stanzas follow a pattern created by the sixteenth-century poet Edmund Spenser and used in his allegorical epic *The Faerie Queene*. Eight lines of iambic pentameter are followed by a ninth line with six feet rather than five (an alexandrine), which has the effect of slowing or drawing out the rhythm. (See Interpretations pages 93–4.)

This is followed by *Choric Song*, in which the drugged mariners – who have themselves now become *Lotos-eaters* – speak in chorus of their desire to abandon the voyage and give in to their addiction. They alternate between praising the attractions of the place and the pleasurable effects of the drug (in odd-numbered stanzas), and complaining about their former lives of hardship and *toil* (in even-numbered stanzas). The stanzas here are irregular, with varied rhythmic and rhyming patterns that mirror these contrasts.

The poem explores a range of ideas about the attractions of addiction, but the form, which is similar to a dramatic monologue, allows the subject to be seen from more than one point of view. The words are those of the addicts, but what is Tennyson's own view of them and their behaviour? Christopher Ricks (see Further Reading page 147) points out a connection with an 'urgent letter' Tennyson wrote in 1831 to a Cambridge friend, W.H. Brookfield, who was addicted to opium:

> What are you about – musing, and brooding and dreaming and opium-eating yourself out of this life into the next?… if you do not [give up the drug] I can foresee nothing for you but stupefaction, aneurism, confusion, horror and death.
>
> Christopher Ricks, *Tennyson*, page 91

First published in 1832, the poem was revised for inclusion in *Poems* (1842).

1–2 **'Courage!'** Ulysses has to encourage his men; are they already weary and reluctant? What is the impact of the opening word, compared to the rest of the poem? This word immediately disrupts poetic rhythm; its energy contrasts with the dreamy, rocking, iambic pattern that follows.

1–3 **land / land** Tennyson said he chose this 'no rhyme' for its 'lazier' effect.

8, 10 **like a downward smoke**   The imagery here is based on
effects Tennyson had seen when visiting a waterfall in the
Pyrenees, France.

  9 **fall and pause and fall**   What is the effect of the rhythm in
this line?
did seem   Why does the poet use this archaic form rather
than 'seemed'?

11 **lawn**   fine, delicate linen or cotton fabric.

13 **slumbrous**   sleepy, drowsy.

18 **Up-clomb**   climbed.
woven copse   tangled bushes and vegetation.

23 **galingale**   sedge; plant similar to marsh grass or rushes.

27 Consider the effect of the 'm' and 'l' sounds in this line. What
impression does it give of the *Lotos-eaters*, compared to their
surroundings?

30 **whoso**   whoever.

38 **Between the sun and moon**   In this land where it is *always
afternoon* (4), the moon has already risen while the sun is still
setting. See lines 7 and 19.

Choric Song

51 **tir'd**   Tennyson commented that the sound of this word
should be 'neither monosyllabic nor disyllabic, but a dreamy
child of the two'. Experiment with reading this line, or the
whole of this stanza, aloud.

60 **toil**   This word is repeated five more times in the poem (61,
69, 82, 166, 171). What is the effect of this?

61 **the first of things**   Humans are supposed to be the most
important and intelligent beings.

66 **steep**   soak. This gives the idea of being able to drown in
sleep.

67 **harken**   listen to.

69 **the roof and crown of things**   See line 61 and Note.

71 **woo'd**   coaxed.

73 **takes no care**   The idea is that all this happens naturally
to the *leaf* – it doesn't need to work or worry in order to
flourish.

78 **waxing over-mellow**   becoming over-ripe.

81–2 The mariners complain that their lives are driven by work and full of distress, while nature just runs its course naturally. This echoes the Bible (Matthew 6:28): 'Consider the lilies of the field, how they grow; they toil not, neither do they spin'.

91–2 Death means that all good things that humans have are taken from them and just become part of the past, so what point is there in chasing after them? The things they used to desire – youth, friends, possessions – have now become *dreadful*.

111–12 **those old faces… mound of grass**   their parents, now dead and buried.

122 **ten years' war in Troy**   See headnote and also Notes on *Ulysses*, page 66.

124 **the little isle**   Ithaca, their home.

132 **pilot-stars**   The stars that sailors use for guidance in setting the course of a ship.

133 **amaranth**   a flower believed to be immortal.
moly   a magically protective herb.

142 **acanthus** flowering plant with jagged-shaped leaves.

143 **brine**   sea.

151 **starboard**   right-hand side of a boat, when facing forward.
larboard   left-hand side of a boat.

153 **with an equal mind**   calmly and steadily.

154 **hollow**   Is this term positive or negative here?

155 **Gods together, careless of mankind**   This view of the gods is based on ideas in the writings of the Roman poet Lucretius, explaining the philosophy of Epicureanism. This teaches that human salvation is not to be found in superstitious beliefs, but by taking pleasure in friendship and a simple way of life. If the gods exist, they are on a completely different level and have no interest in the human race.

160–61 Explore the effect of these lines by reading them aloud.

163 **Steaming up**   The sounds of earth rise like steam.

165 **cleave**   plough.

167 **little dues**   small harvests.

169 **Elysian valleys**   In Greek mythology, Elysium is heaven, or the final resting place of the heroic and virtuous after death.

170 **asphodel**   plant with white or yellow flowers. English poets, including Milton, describe the fields of Elysium as being carpeted with asphodel.

Ulysses

The mythological hero Ulysses (or Odysseus), ruler of the Greek island of Ithaca, features in two great epic poems by the Greek poet Homer. The *Iliad* tells the story of the Trojan War, which resulted from the abduction of the Greek queen Helen of Sparta by Paris, Prince of Troy. Ulysses has a prominent role as a heroic fighter and leader. The *Odyssey* relates his adventures on the journey home, which lasted 10 years and involved all kinds of dangers, including encounters with the one-eyed Cyclops and the seductive Sirens. He and his companions faced and escaped the terrors of the Underworld, and Ulysses also managed to free them from the addictive pleasure-giving drugs of the Lotus-Eaters (see page 62). However, when his sailors disobey divine laws, the ship is wrecked as a punishment and only Ulysses survives.

On his return to Ithaca after an absence of 20 years, Ulysses finds that his *aged wife* (3), Penelope, has remained faithful to him, but is under pressure from many suitors to marry again. He deals with these interlopers and restores order to his kingdom.

Tennyson's poem forms a sort of epilogue or sequel to these adventures. Having remained *idle* (1) in Ithaca for three years, Ulysses is restless and ready for more action. He is old now, but nevertheless his *hungry heart* (12) *cannot rest from travel* (6). He plans to leave the business of ruling Ithaca to his son, Telemachus, who seems to be home-loving and more suited to the task. A ship is being prepared, and he invites his men to join him in a final voyage in which *Some work of noble note, may yet be done* (52) before they die.

The idea is suggested in the *Odyssey* Book 11, when it is foretold that Ulysses will go on a final voyage where he will meet his death. Another source is Dante's *Inferno*. Ulysses speaks to his men:

> 'O brothers!' I began, 'who to the west
> 'Through perils without number now have reach'd,
> 'To this the short remaining watch, that yet
> 'Our senses have to wake...

'Call to mind from whence ye sprang:
'Ye were not form'd to live the life of brutes,
'But virtue to pursue and knowledge high.'
With these few words I sharpen'd for the voyage
The mind of my associates...
(Dante's *Inferno*, Book 26, 113–122, translated by H.F. Cary)

This is echoed by Tennyson, who uses the form of a dramatic monologue (see Interpretations page 111) in which Ulysses speaks to his *mariners* (45), his old friends and companions (although, according to the *Odyssey*, they had all perished).

Tennyson wrote *Ulysses* in October 1833, very soon after receiving the news that his friend Arthur Hallam had died. He said later that it was 'written under the sense of loss and that all had gone by, but that still life must be fought out to the end'. Critics have often pointed out that the poem has an ambiguous or paradoxical quality. Although Ulysses' words express his need for further adventure and his belief that his life of action is not over, other qualities in the poem suggest quite a different feeling. The pace and rhythm are not fast and urgent, but slow; and, strangely, the future tense is hardly used at all. The effect is to create a feeling of weariness or reluctance, which pulls against the surface meaning. Can we fully believe him? See also Notes to lines 19–21, 54–61 and 62–3.

1–5   What is Ulysses' tone here? What does his vocabulary tell us about his attitude to his home, his country and his people? What does the word *me* (5) suggest about him?
  3   **mete and dole**   administer and give out.
  4   **Unequal laws**   unfair laws, 'not affecting all in the same manner or degree' (according to Tennyson).
  5   **sleep, and feed**   This echoes Shakespeare's *Hamlet* IV.iv.33–5: 'What is a man / If his chief good and market of his time / Be but to sleep and feed? A beast, no more.'
  7   **lees**   deposits left at the bottom of a vat (or glass) of wine. Ulysses means he wants to make the most of life – to 'drink' it to the very last drop.

Notes

- 10 **Hyades**   Five nymphs associated with the stars known as the Hyades, part of the larger constellation Taurus, associated with the coming of rain.
- 19–21 The poet Matthew Arnold suggested that 'these three lines by themselves take up nearly as much time as a whole book of the *Iliad*'.
- 23 **unburnish'd**   not polished. The metaphor suggests his desire to be like a well-used sword, shining and involved in the action – not a rusty one.
- 29 **three suns**   three years.
- 31 **sinking star**   This ambiguous phrase could suggest either seeking out the unknown, which is beyond the horizon, like the stars that appear to 'sink' or 'set' into the sea as the earth turns; or that Ulysses feels himself to be nearing the end of his life and wishes to gain as much knowledge as he can in the time that remains.
- 33–43 Look at the vocabulary used to describe Telemachus here. How does Tennyson bring out the contrast between Ulysses and his son in these lines?
- 33–4 Ulysses explains that he plans to leave the business of ruling Ithaca (*the isle*) in the hands of his son Telemachus; the *sceptre* is a ceremonial staff, a symbol of authority.
- 42 **household gods**   deities or spirits that protect the home. Ulysses suggests that his son will treat these with suitable respect and take good care of his home and family in his absence.
- 44 He points out the harbour, where a ship is already being prepared for their departure.
- 45 **My mariners**   It becomes clear that Ulysses' words are addressed to the sailors and companions who have accompanied him on his previous adventures – although, according to the *Odyssey*, they all perished on the previous journey home (see headnote).
- 47–8 **with a frolic welcome… and the sunshine**   They have always happily welcomed both good and bad experiences.
- 48–9 **opposed / Free hearts, free foreheads**   acted of their own free will.
- 53 **men that strove with Gods**   Their mythical adventures involved overcoming challenges set by hostile gods, with the support of more friendly deities.

54–61 Read these lines aloud. Notice the vocabulary and pace. Do you think Ulysses' words are convincing here?

58–9 **Push off… sounding furrows** Ulysses urges his men to push out the boat, get organized as a crew and start rowing; *smite* (hit forcefully) suggests the energy with which he wants their oars to strike the waves (*furrows*).

60–61 **To sail… the western stars** He wants to sail beyond the horizon, where the sun sets and the stars seem to vanish into the sea (see also line 31 and Note).

62–3 The future tense is used here (see headnote) – but notice the repeated, indefinite *may be*.

63 **Happy Isles** the 'Isles of the Blest' of Greek mythology, or heaven. They may die in this venture.

64 **Achilles** hero of Homer's *Iliad* and comrade of Ulysses, who was killed during the Trojan War.

68 This suggests he and his men all share the same objective – as if their hearts beat as one.

70 The poem's final line was engraved as a permanent installation in the centre of the Olympic Village for the London 2012 Olympics, to inspire the athletes. Do you think it was a good choice?

Godiva

Lady Godiva was an Anglo-Saxon noblewoman, married to Leofric, Earl of Mercia, one of the most powerful noblemen in eleventh-century England. She is still revered in the city of Coventry today because of a legend that tells how she sympathized with the people of the town when they were suffering terribly under the ruthless taxation levied by her husband. She appealed to him to show compassion, and was so persistent that eventually he became exasperated and said he would abolish the taxes if she would ride naked through the town. She took up the challenge and, after issuing an order that everyone in Coventry was to stay inside with all doors and windows barred, she rode across the town with only her long hair for covering. Leofric kept his word and cancelled the extortionate taxes. In a later addition to the story, one man who was unable to resist spying on her bored a hole in his window shutters, but was struck blind when he looked out; he was the original 'peeping Tom'.

Tennyson's re-telling of the story was written after a visit to Coventry in June 1840, and published in *Poems* (1842). It may have been influenced by an earlier version of *Godiva* by John Moultrie (1799–1874), which would have been known to Tennyson. According to his friend William Ewart Gladstone (who later became prime minister), the poem shows signs of an 'increasing growth of ethical and social wisdom' in Tennyson.

The Pre-Raphaelite artist John Collier painted a picture of Lady Godiva in about 1898 (see Interpretations page 104).

1–4   This narrative 'frame', which introduces the legend, was criticized by Leigh Hunt (a poet and essayist who had been a friend of the poets Keats and Shelley). He accused Tennyson of trying to manipulate the reader's opinion by adopting a 'mixed tone of contempt and nonchalance', as if pretending the poem is a 'trifle' and that he doesn't care how we receive it. 'There is a boyishness in this which we shall be happy to see Mr Tennyson, who is no longer a boy, outgrow.'

   3   **three tall spires**   Coventry is known as the city of the three spires, which belong to the old Cathedral and two of the city's main churches, although it is not easy to see all three at once.

   5   **latest seed of Time**   most recent, most modern people.

   6   **flying of a wheel**   Tennyson is referring to the speed of travel on the new railway.

   7   **Cry down**   criticize.
       prate   preach, talk at length.

18–19   **His beard... yard behind**   What image of the Earl do these lines create?

   24   **by Peter and by Paul**   by Saint Peter and Saint Paul.

   25   **fillip'd at**   flicked.

   28   **as rough as Esau's hand**   This is a reference to the Bible story in Genesis 27. Of the two sons of Isaac, Esau, the elder, had hairy hands, hardened by outdoor work, in contrast with his brother Jacob, whose hands were smooth.

36–7 **cry... hard condition**   announce, with a blast of his trumpet, the terms that have been laid down.

37 **loose**   set free.

43 **wedded eagles**   decorative clasps shaped like eagles.

51 **palfrey**   well-bred horse, considered suitable for women to ride.

trapt   equipped.

53 **clothed on with chastity**   i.e. her chastity, or modesty, is her only garment. Note the repetition in line 65. Why is this idea repeated?

56 **heads upon the spout**   carved heads decorating the fountain.

64 **the Gothic archway in the wall**   the town gate.

66 **low churl, compact of thankless earth**   rude, mean-spirited person, of low birth.

67 **fatal byword**   unfortunate figure of speech (i.e. 'Peeping Tom').

68 **auger-hole**   drill-hole.

71 **Powers**   gods.

72 **cancell'd**   destroyed, took away. 'Peeping Tom' is struck blind for misusing his *sense* of sight.

74 **shameless noon**   In what ways might the noon be *shameless* here?

'Break, break, break'

This poem is an expression of grief at the death of Tennyson's friend Arthur Hallam (see page 8 and Notes on *In Memoriam*, page 75). It was written between 1833 and 1837, and first published in *Poems* (1842). Here, deep feeling is expressed in simple, restrained language. The poet watches an everyday seaside scene unfolding around him, contrasting with and intensifying his sense of loss.

For a nineteenth-century critic's view of this poem, see Interpretations pages 107–8.

1 **Break, break, break**   Where are these words directed? Does
your perception of this alter as you read the following lines?
Literally, these words are addressed to the waves, but is he
also describing his heart – and his feeling of being unable to
articulate, and so release, his sorrow?

2 **cold gray stones**   Like the *crags* in line 14, this phrase
suggests harsh reality, and that nature is indifferent to his grief.

5–12 What is the effect of the repeated O and the exclamation
marks? Compare the impact of the exclamations in stanza 2
with lines 11–12.

14–15 Note the contrasting language in these lines.

The Princess

'Tears, idle tears' and *'Now sleeps the crimson petal'* are taken
from *The Princess.* In this long dramatic poem, Tennyson tackles
questions about relations between the sexes and the role of
women in society. In particular, he explores the contemporary
issue of the higher education of women. The idea first came to
him in the late 1830s and Hallam Tennyson suggests that it may
have been sparked by a discussion with Emily Sellwood; 'the
project of a Womens' College' was in his mind, although the
first college to award academic qualifications to women, Queen's
College, London, did not open until 1848.

Although the subject matter is serious, it is presented in a
semi-comic, satirical manner, and, taken as a whole, the resulting
poem is rather equivocal and has been called 'unsatisfactory'. It
is a strange tale, made up of sometimes rather disparate parts
and interspersed with some beautiful songs. Tennyson called it
a 'medley', pointing to the way he has placed the central plot
within a frame: seven students decide to invent a story to amuse
themselves, each taking turns to contribute part of the narrative.

The story they tell concerns a princess who rejects the world
of men, including the prince to whom she is engaged, to found
a university for women only. She claims that women are 'twice

as quick' as men and that only 'convention beats them down'. Men are excluded 'on pain of death'. The prince and two friends disguise themselves as women and join the university, which is rather stereotypically feminine, with 'beauties every shade of brown and fair / In colours gayer than the morning mist'. They all ride out into the countryside, raise 'a tent of satin' and have a feast and entertainment. One of the young women sings *'Tears, idle tears'*. The men are discovered when one of them sings a bawdy song; the women run away, but the princess falls into the river and has to be rescued by the prince. She still declares that the men must die, which causes a battle between an army sent by the prince's father and one provided by her brother. The university is turned into a hospital to deal with the casualties; the princess nurses the prince, and reads *'Now sleeps the crimson petal'* at his bedside. She falls in love with him and they are married in a traditional happy ending.

W.S. Gilbert used the poem as the basis for a farcical musical drama in 1870 and then, in collaboration with Arthur Sullivan, turned it into the popular comic opera *Princess Ida*, first performed in 1884.

When the poem was published in 1847, Tennyson's friends were disappointed with the work. Edward FitzGerald thought it was a waste of his talent and called it a 'grotesque abortion', while Thomas Carlyle wrote that it contained 'everything but common sense'. More recent critics suggest that he did not do justice to the subject: 'The University is presented as little more than a second-rate girls' school... The whole subject of female education has been so trivialized as almost to dismiss its seriousness' (Robert Bernard Martin, *Tennyson: The Unquiet Heart*, page 312).

It is useful to bear in mind, however, that feminism was a very new idea when Tennyson was writing, and it was unusual to engage with these issues at all.

There is no doubt that Tennyson's skill with language is as apparent in *The Princess* as in any of his other work. The two songs included here are considered to be among his finest short lyrics.

'Tears, idle tears'

One of the young women of the university sings this song to entertain her companions.

Tennyson was quoted in the literary magazine *The Nineteenth Century* as saying: 'This song came to me... at Tintern Abbey, full for me of its bygone memories. It is the sense of abiding in the transient.' He also said, 'It is what I have always felt even from a boy, and what as a boy I called the "passion of the past". And it is so always with me now; it is the distance that charms me in the landscape, the picture and the past, and not the immediate day in which I move.'

'Now sleeps the crimson petal'

The prince, half asleep, but 'Fill'd thro' and thro' with Love', hears the princess read this short poem to him, while she nurses him after the battle.

It is in the form of a *ghazal*, an ancient, traditional type of love poetry from Persia (now Iran) and India, which was popular with some European writers, especially in Germany, during the nineteenth century. Conventionally, this consists of a series of couplets, with the same metre in each line. Every few lines, a final word is repeated, creating a form of rhyme; here, the word is *me*. The subject matter is also traditional: erotic love, usually for someone unattainable. There are 'stock' recurring images: roses, lilies, cypress trees, peacocks, stars.

   3 **porphyry**   hard stone of a dark, purplish-red colour.
   7 **Danaë**   In Greek mythology, King Acrisius of Argos was warned by an oracle that he would be killed by a son of his daughter Danaë, so he shut Danaë in a bronze room, and kept her away from all male company. However, Zeus fell in love with her, and as Tennyson put it, 'came down to Danaë when shut up in the tower in a shower of golden stars', and she bore a son, Perseus.

In Memoriam A.H.H.

Tennyson gave *In Memoriam A.H.H.* the sub-heading *OBIIT MDCCCXXXIII* ('Died 1833'). It is a sequence of 133 short poems that explore the experience of bereavement and of a gradual coming to terms with loss. The poems were written in response to the death of Tennyson's friend Arthur Henry Hallam, and were composed over a period of 17 years, between Hallam's death in 1833 and the publication of the collection in 1850.

It was in October 1833 that Tennyson received the devastating news that Hallam, his closest friend, had died suddenly while travelling abroad with his father (see also page 8). At one blow, Tennyson had lost the prospect of a crucial, lifelong friendship and what his brother Charles described as 'The prop, round which his own growth had twined itself for four fruitful years'.

Tennyson may well have idealized his friend, who died full of promise at the age of 23; but if so, he was not alone. William Ewart Gladstone, who was a school friend of Hallam and went on to become the most prominent politician and prime minister of the Victorian age, gives the impression that Hallam was almost worshipped by his contemporaries: 'It is the simple truth that Arthur Henry Hallam was a spirit so exceptional that everything with which he was brought into relation during his shortened passage through this world came to be, through this contact, glorified by a touch of the ideal' (interview in the *Daily Telegraph*, 5 January 1898).

Although Tennyson was crushed by this loss, which reinforced the suffering he had experienced in his family and magnified his tendency to despair and bitterness, he began almost immediately to put his feelings into words, in short lyric poems he called 'elegies'.

When he began the 'earliest jottings' in 1833, he did not initially 'write them with any view of weaving them into a whole, or for publication, until I found that I had written so many'. But over the years, he continued to add more poems, and eventually organized and edited the collection to give it a more definite and meaningful structure. Although the poems explore so many different facets of his experience, they are united by the use of a common stanza pattern: four lines of iambic tetrameter, with the rhyme scheme *abba*. See Interpretations pages 104–7.

Tennyson sometimes referred to the work as *The Way of the Soul*, but the chosen title, *In Memoriam A.H.H.*, was suggested by his wife-to-be, Emily Sellwood. As in some other famous memorial poems, such as John Milton's *Lycidas* (1637), the basic movement is from grief and loss to a sense of new and greater life, but here the impression is of a gradual and difficult process that lasts several years. Roughly speaking, the poems are arranged so that they seem to cover a period of around three years, with different stages marked by the seasons and by anniversaries such as Christmas.

A.C. Bradley, in his *Commentary on Tennyson's In Memoriam* sums up the 'way of the soul' as:

> a journey from the first stupor and confusion of grief, through a growing acquiescence often disturbed by the recurrence of pain, to an almost unclouded peace and joy... The soul, at first almost sunk in the feeling of loss, finds itself at last freed from regret and yet strengthened in affection... The world which once seemed to it a mere echo of its sorrow, has become the abode of that immortal Love, at once divine and human, which includes the living and the dead.
>
> (*A Commentary on Tennyson's In Memoriam*, 1901, page 27)

However, the journey is not straightforward; along the way, Tennyson explores some of the biggest questions of his day. For example, how do you hold onto religious beliefs and a sense of meaning in life, when scientific discoveries seem to contradict your faith?

In Memoriam was extremely popular in the nineteenth century and was a favourite of Queen Victoria, who found solace in it after the death of her husband, Prince Albert.

V

In the early part of the sequence, the poet is numb and disbelieving. Here, he wonders whether it is appropriate to try to make poetry about his grief, since words can never do justice to his feelings. However, he decides that even the process of composing with *measured* rhyme and rhythm is useful as it helps to deaden his pain, and he can use words as a protective shield.

   6 **measured language**   poetry, with regular rhyme and rhythm.
   8 **narcotics**   drugs derived from the opium poppy, which dull the sense of pain and cause drowsiness or sleep.
   9 **weeds**   clothes (archaic). The word was most commonly used for the black clothes worn when mourning a death, as in the phrase 'widow's weeds'.
11–12 Compare Shakespeare's *Hamlet*, I.ii.85–6: 'But I have that within which passes show, / These but the trappings and the suits of woe'.
  12 **outline**   The idea is of a line drawing or sketch, which does not fill in the detail or colour of the image; his words are on the outside, like clothes, and do not reveal his inner feelings.

VII

Unable to sleep, he visits his friend's empty house at dawn, as if unable to believe he is no longer there. (See Essay Questions pages 138–9 for a contrasting poem.)

   1 **Dark house**   Hallam had lived at 67 Wimpole Street, London.
   7 **like a guilty thing I creep**   It is as if he is ashamed to be seen there, and ashamed of the strength of his feelings. This echoes *Hamlet* I.i.153, where the ghost of Hamlet's father 'started like a guilty thing' when it was discovered.
   9 **He is not here**   Note the devastatingly simple, bald statement. What does it convey – disappointment? Weary resignation?
     far away   i.e. in busier streets. They may not in reality be so far away, but the world of life and business feels very distant to the grieving poet.

11–12   These lines convey a sense of utter desolation. Which words and poetic techniques contribute most to this effect?

XXIV

Now he wonders whether the past was really perfect, or whether it only seems so because it contrasts so strongly with the present. Or does time always lend enchantment to the past, making it appear rosier than it was?

3   **source and fount of Day**   i.e. the sun.
4   **wandering isles of night**   sun spots. Nothing is perfect; even the sun is flawed and has dark patches.
5–8   This stanza questions the previous poem in the sequence, XXIII, in which he remembers the happy companionship he enjoyed with Hallam, when they could almost read each other's minds:

And Thought leapt out to wed with Thought
　　Ere Thought could wed itself with Speech;
And all we met was fair and good,
　　And all was good that Time could bring

But now he thinks it could never have been this good. The human race has never fully appreciated the goodness life has to offer: even in *Paradise* (6), the Garden of Eden, Eve was dissatisfied, wanting more, and therefore open to temptation.

9   **haze**   The present is clouded by unhappiness.
12   **sets the past in this relief**   makes the past stand out in contrast to the present. In sculpture, a design in relief is carved so that it stands out from the surrounding background.
15   **orb**   turn or change.

L

This famous poem belongs to a group in which the poet explores the idea of the continued existence of the dead. He feels sickness, pain and evil in himself and in the world, which causes him to question whether life has meaning and to doubt his faith in God and in love. He expresses his feelings more passionately, longing for some sort of reassuring contact with his friend in the present.

Here, the words are addressed directly to his friend, in the form of a prayer, asking that he will be present with him when he is in pain, depressed and at the time of death.

2–3 What is the effect of the rhyme, enjambment and punctuation in these lines?

4 **wheels of Being** processes of living. He feels *slow*ed down, physically and mentally.

5 **sensuous frame** physical body, which feels through the senses.

8 **a Fury slinging flame** In Roman mythology, the Furies were goddesses of vengeance, sometimes depicted carrying deadly flaming torches.

10–12 This metaphor compares human life to that of a short-lived fly. He may be referring to the mayfly, an insect with a very short lifespan. How would you describe the feeling and tone here? What is he suggesting about life?

11 **sting and sing** What is the effect of this internal rhyme?

12 **weave their petty cells** make their tiny and pathetic nests.

14 **point the term** show or mark the end.

15 **verge** limit or edge. This suggests he imagines being right on the brink of death.

LXVII

By this phase of *In Memoriam*, there is a sense that the poet's grief is beginning to soften. Here again, he addresses his friend directly. The moonlight shining in his window connects them, as he imagines the same light falling on his friend's grave. When this *glory* (4, 9) fades, and darkness falls, he sleeps until dawn; the connection remains, in the mist that stretches across the country.

2 **place of rest** Arthur Hallam was buried in the aisle of St Andrews Church, Clevedon, Somerset, where he had family connections. Tennyson had not seen the grave – he did not visit Clevedon until 1850, the year in which *In Memoriam* was published.

3 **broad water of the west** the Bristol Channel, where Clevedon is situated.
5 **marble** tomb or gravestone.
11 **eaves** This image connects him with the church, as he compares his eyelids closing to the shadow falling over the eaves (the overhanging edges) of the church roof.
14 **lucid veil** Is this an oxymoron? It suggests a veil that hides, yet is clear and bright.
16 **tablet** gravestone.

CVI

At this stage, the poet has moved to a new home and commemorates the third Christmas and New Year since the death of his friend. Tennyson wrote this poem at New Year 1837–8, when his family had just moved from Lincolnshire to Epping Forest, in Essex.

As the bells ring in celebration of the New Year, he turns away from the past, letting go of the personal grief that has *sap*ped his *mind* (9), but not of his love for his friend. Instead, this love continues to grow, becoming universal rather than individual. The friend comes to symbolize his hopeful vision for the future: that the human race will become more noble, peaceful, honest, loving and courageous.

1 **Ring out, wild bells** Church bells are traditionally rung at midnight on December 31 to signal and welcome the New Year.
4 **him** i.e. the old year.
9 **saps** drains, weakens.
12 **redress** remedy, justice.
14 **party strife** conflict or squabbling between political parties.
17 **want** need, poverty.
care worry, trouble.
18 **coldness** indifference, lack of human warmth and sympathy.
20 **fuller minstrel** better – and perhaps happier – poet or musician.
21 **place and blood** position in society and belonging to an aristocratic family.

22 **civic** political. This suggests politicians unfairly criticizing, or telling insulting lies about, each other.

26 **narrowing lust of gold** desire for money that makes people mean and narrow-minded.

27–8 In the Bible, Revelation 20:2–4 foretells that Satan will be 'bound… a thousand years, and cast… into the bottomless pit, and shut… up' with 'a seal upon him, that he should deceive the nations no more, till the thousand years should be fulfilled'.

32 According to his son, Tennyson

> expressed his conviction… that the forms of Christian religion would alter, but that the spirit of Christ would still grow from more to more 'in the roll of the ages',
> Till each man find his own in all men's good,
> And all men work in noble brotherhood
> when Christianity without bigotry will triumph, when the controversies of creeds shall have vanished…
>
> (Hallam Tennyson, *Alfred, Lord Tennyson: A Memoir*, Volume I, page 325)

CXV

Nearing the end of the sequence, the poet finds he can once more rejoice in the beauty of life and nature. In this poignant poem, Hallam Tennyson explained, 'Spring comes once more, and with the beauty of the world his regret also awakes and blossoms'. His sadness and *regret* (18) have not disappeared, but have been changed. There is a sense of relief, in the final stanza, as it seems he feels once more part of the world and in tune with nature.

2 **burgeons** puts forth new shoots; flourishes; grows rapidly.
maze of quick tangled hedge of quickset thorn, or hawthorn.

4 **ashen** of ash trees; but perhaps also of pale colour.

8 **sightless** invisible. Compare P.B. Shelley, *To a Skylark*: 'Like a star of heaven, / In the broad daylight / Thou art unseen, but yet I hear thy shrill delight'.

9 **lea** meadow, field.

13 **seamew**   seagull.
15–17 **change their sky... land to land**   These lines describe the
seasonal migration of birds.
19 **April violet**   The violet has several symbolic meanings: it
has been used to suggest humility and modesty, mourning
or spiritual wisdom. In Shelley's poem *On a Faded Violet*, it
symbolizes grief for a lost love.

The Charge of the Light Brigade

In November 1854, Tennyson read reports in *The Times* of a
disastrous incident during the Battle of Balaclava, in the Crimean
War, where British, French and Turkish forces were involved
in trying to capture the Russian naval base at Sevastopol. A
'hideous blunder' over a misunderstood order sent over 600
lightly armed cavalrymen (soldiers on horseback) into a valley
where they were greatly outnumbered and an easy target for the
Russian guns. Over two thirds of the men were killed, injured or
taken prisoner.

Tennyson was very struck not only by their bravery in
following orders without question, but also by the futility of their
sacrifice. According to Hallam Tennyson's *Memoir* (Volume I,
page 381), he wrote the whole poem almost immediately and 'in a
few minutes'. In his mind, the phrase 'hideous blunder' from the
newspaper became *Some one had blunder'd* (12), which provided
the basis for the poem's galloping dactylic rhythm. (A dactyl is a
metrical foot consisting of one stressed syllable followed by two
unstressed ones.) Later, Tennyson did not consider it one of his
better poems.

In 1890, Tennyson agreed to have his voice recorded onto a
wax phonograph cylinder for Thomas Edison. You can hear this
recording of him reading *The Charge of the Light Brigade* via the
BBC Arts web page http://www.bbc.co.uk/arts/poetry/outloud/
tennyson.shtml

Title **Light Brigade**   The brigade was made up of five battalions of light cavalry troops, lightly armed and lightly armoured men mounted on lightly armoured horses, led by the Earl of Cardigan.

   1 **league**   distance of about three miles.

5–6 This is Tennyson's interpretation of the confused order.

   7 **the valley of Death**   This is the name the soldiers gave it, according to *The Times*.

 17 **hundred**   The word was pronounced 'hunderd' in Lincolnshire, so the rhyme is complete.

18–20 Russian guns were placed ahead and on each side of the valley.

 27 **sabres**   long, curved swords.

 32 **battery**   organized group of guns.

 34 **Cossack**   soldier from territories on the borders of the Russian Empire; they were often skilled horsemen.

Maud

Maud, which was originally subtitled *The Madness*, explores, through fiction, some themes from Tennyson's own earlier life: a family tainted with hereditary madness; frustrated love; loss and disappointment. Later, the poem was given the heading *A Monodrama*. As in a dramatic monologue, the words are spoken by one character; but the drama is built out of a number of short poems in varied forms, which portray different episodes in the story and different moods. Tennyson liked to read this poem aloud, and said of it: 'The peculiarity of this poem is that different phases of passion in one person take the place of different characters'. He also described it as 'a little *Hamlet*', although the plot has more echoes of *Romeo and Juliet*.

In Part I the speaker, a young man who is never named, begins by raging against the 'villainy' of the world. He loves Maud, the beautiful daughter of a neighbouring family, but they are divided by a feud. Corruption has led to his father's bankruptcy and suicide, and has made her family immensely rich, at the expense of his own. They fall in love despite the situation, but Maud's proud brother objects, treating the speaker with 'scorn'. He and Maud have a romantic meeting in the garden of his former family home – which now belongs to hers.

Part II reveals that the speaker has escaped to France after killing Maud's brother in a duel. However, he is haunted by her ghost and when he learns that she has died of grief, he has a mental breakdown and is imprisoned in an asylum.

In Part III, the speaker claims that his 'mood is changed' and he has recovered his sanity. Maud has appeared to him in a dream, urging him to join the army and go to war in the Crimea. Now in a 'better mind', he goes off to 'fight for the good' and 'embrace the purpose of God'.

The starting point for the poem was the earlier lyric *O that t'were possible* (line 1 of this extract), but Tennyson worked on *Maud* during 1854 and the complete poem was published in 1855. It received a mixed response; some considered it morbid, and Tennyson was accused of glorifying war. William Ewart Gladstone, who was initially critical of the poem's 'war-frenzy', subsequently accepted Tennyson's explanation that this was a 'work of imagination' with a fictional speaker.

Part II, no. IV

Originally written much earlier, in 1833–4, this was another expression of his grief following the loss of Arthur Hallam, though the male figure has been replaced by a young woman. This forms the core of Part II of *Maud*. The speaker, now in France and on the verge of breakdown, longs to be reunited with Maud, who haunts him in dreams and visions. He reminisces about their meeting in the garden and describes his misery and alienation in the foreign city.

20–22   In his fragile emotional state, the noise and busyness of the world is overwhelming. In *Maud*, Tennyson alludes several times to life in the industrialized city – see also lines 63–72 and 89–94 in this extract, and also Part V, which follows.

56 **Get thee hence**   go away. See the Bible, Matthew 4:10, where
Jesus is tempted by the devil and says 'Get thee hence, Satan';
this would have been normal usage in Shakespeare's time, but
archaic in the nineteenth century.

58 **type**   symbol, representative (archaic).

63–72 How does Tennyson use language to present the city
in these lines? Compare the way he describes the
narrator's memory of the garden where he met Maud, in
lines 31–43.

Part II, no. V

These lines, which follow on from the previous extract, are set in
the asylum in France. Here the speaker has lost touch with reality
and experiences himself as being dead and buried in a shallow
grave, tormented by the life going on above him and the *dead* that
surround him. Hallam Tennyson reports: 'About the mad-scene
one of the best-known doctors for the insane wrote that it was
"the most faithful representation of madness since Shakespeare"'
(*A Memoir*, Volume I, page 398).

1–5 Read these lines aloud. Consider the effects of the metre and
rhythm here, and also of the repetition (anaphora) of *And* in
lines 3–5.

7 In his delusion, he feels as if he has died and been buried, but
not deeply enough. A few stanzas later, he complains that in
this 'Wretchedest age' even gravediggers cannot do their job
properly:

O me, why have they not buried me deep enough?
Is it kind to have made me a grave so rough,
Me, that was never a quiet sleeper?
(*Maud*, Part II, no. V, lines 96–8)

12 What image and feeling is created in this line?

20 The stanza ends with the only full stop in the extract. What is
the effect of the punctuation in this extract?

Tithonus

Humans have always aspired to conquer death and achieve immortality. In this dramatic monologue, Tennyson explores the idea that eternal life might not be a blessing after all.

According to a legend told in an ancient Greek hymn, Aurora (or Eos), the goddess of the dawn, fell in love with Tithonus, a prince of Troy. Relationships between mortal humans and immortal deities were always problematic: she asked Zeus to grant Tithonus eternal life, but forgot to request also that he should have eternal youth. Thus while she dawns fresh and blooming every morning, he is doomed to wither away, trapped in endless old age, until he longs for death to end his torment. In some versions of the myth, he is eventually turned into a cicada or grasshopper, but Tennyson leaves the situation unresolved.

Tennyson wrote an early version, *Tithon*, in 1833 in the aftermath of Arthur Hallam's death, intending it to be a companion piece to *Ulysses*, but it was never published. It is considered to reflect his grief and fears about mortality, particularly the idea that through premature death, Hallam would remain eternally young and so achieve immortality of a kind, while those left behind went forward into old age. Later, their friend Benjamin Jowett visited Hallam's grave and wrote to Tennyson: 'It is a strange feeling about those who are taken young that while we are getting old and dusty they are as they were'.

In 1859, William Thackeray asked Tennyson to contribute a poem for his new magazine *The Cornhill*. Tennyson chose to revise and expand his earlier poem, and *Tithonus* appeared in the magazine in this form in February 1860.

> 2 **burthen** burden (the mist falls as rain), but also the refrain or chorus to a song.
> 4 **dies the swan** The swan has a relatively long lifespan and its whiteness was thought to suggest the white hair of old age; also, according to legend, the swan remains mute until the moment before death, when it sings one beautiful song.

5–6 **Me only... Consumes** In what way is this phrase surprising? Would 'cruel mortality' be more predictable? See also line 70.

18 **strong Hours** In Greek mythology, the Horae, or Hours, were goddesses of the seasons, and controlled the natural divisions of time.

25 **silver star** Venus. When the planet Venus appears in the east before sunrise, as if heralding the dawn, it is known as the morning star.

29 **vary** be different.

30 **goal of ordinance** appointed time.

31 **all should pause** The narrator stresses that everything must die. **most meet** entirely appropriate.

39 **blind the stars** As the dawn breaks, the stars become invisible.

39–41 **the wild team... loosen'd manes** Aurora or Eos is often depicted in a chariot drawn across the sky by radiant horses.

47–9 **lest a saying... recall their gifts** Tithonus is afraid that although Aurora was able to grant him eternal life, she does not have the power to take it away and let him die.

52 **if I be he that watch'd** Remembering the past, he can hardly believe he is the same person.

62–3 **Apollo sing... into towers** Apollo, the sun god, is said to have sung beautiful melodies while the city of Ilion, or Troy, was being built; Tithonus compares these to the *wild and sweet* songs Aurora sang to him in his youth.

64–7 In the *East*, where dawn is always fresh and new, the contrast with his aged body is even more unbearable.

70 See lines 5–6 and Note.

71 **barrows** burial mounds or graves.

76 **silver wheels** i.e. of her chariot (see lines 39–42).

Crossing the Bar

In the summer of 1889, Tennyson was recovering from a serious illness. The nurse who had been caring for him suggested he could write a hymn of thanksgiving. In October, he wrote the poem on a scrap of paper, on board ship, during the return journey from the mainland to his home on the Isle of Wight.

> That evening Nurse Durham came into his study to light the candles and found him sitting alone in the dark. 'Will this do for you, old woman?' he asked gruffly and recited the poem. Forgetting that she had asked him for a hymn of thanksgiving, she thought that he had been overtired by the journey and had composed his own death song; in her agitation she fled without replying, leaving him in the dark room. Later that night he read the poem to Hallam, who said with justice, 'That is one of the most beautiful poems ever written.'
> (Robert Bernard Martin, *Tennyson: The Unquiet Heart*, page 570)

On his deathbed, the poet requested that *Crossing the Bar* should appear at the end of all editions of his poems.

Title **Bar**   sandbank across the mouth of a harbour.

2   This suggests the *call* that summons a sailor to duty – or here, a person to God.

3   **no moaning of the bar**   no noise of waves or shifting sands. But the word *moaning* also suggests the sounds of mourning.

5–8   These lines describe the still point at which the tide turns from incoming to outgoing.

7   **boundless deep**   Tennyson used this phrase to describe the sea on several occasions.

9   **evening bell**   bell that summons people to evening prayer, or vespers.

13   **bourne**   limit, boundary.

15   **Pilot**   i.e. God. A pilot helps guide ships past the sandbank. 'The Pilot has been on board all the while, but in the dark I have not seen him', Tennyson is quoted as saying. His son Hallam said: 'He explained the "Pilot" as "that Divine and Unseen Who is always guiding us"'.
       face to face   This phrase echoes the Bible, 1 Corinthians 13:12: 'For now we see through a glass, darkly; but then face to face'.

Interpretations

Approaching Tennyson's poetry

On one occasion, Tennyson embarrassed a group of listeners (including the eminent writer Thomas Carlyle) at a dinner party by saying: 'I don't think that since Shakespeare there has been such a master of the English language as I' – but then he made them laugh by adding, humorously, 'To be sure, I've got nothing to say'. That was an exaggeration, of course, but it makes a useful point. The artistic aspects of poetry – form, technique and beauty in the use of language – were very important to Tennyson. His skill was so highly regarded that he was described by one admirer in the *Edinburgh Review* as 'the champion who rescued the lost Lady of Style'. It is important that in studying his work we do not get so caught up in the details of his craftsmanship and artistry with language that we neglect to think about what he is saying and the effect his work has on us.

The critic A.C. Bradley, in his *Commentary on Tennyson's In Memoriam* (1901), distinguished between two ways of approaching the study of poetry. 'Interpretation', on the one hand, is thinking about the possible meanings of poems. What is the poet saying? What is described? What ideas and messages are expressed? 'Aesthetic criticism', on the other hand, is the study of a poet's artistry in using the techniques of poetry and the effectiveness and beauty of these. To study or write about poetry successfully, we need to think about both of these and the interrelationships between them.

Before his premature death, Arthur Hallam wrote a review in which he pointed out several features that made his friend Tennyson's poetry stand out, even very early in his career. Two of these are particularly important. First, his ability to describe things in a special, emotionally charged way:

> his vivid, picturesque delineation of objects, and the peculiar skill with which he holds all of them *fused* – to borrow a metaphor from science, in a medium of strong emotion.

And secondly, his command of a wide range of poetic forms:

> the variety of his lyrical measures, and the exquisite
> modulation of harmonious words and cadences to the swell
> and fall of the feelings expressed.

Tennyson's descriptive power

Tennyson's remark that he was the greatest master of the English language since Shakespeare was made in jest, but there was some truth to his claim. Close study of his work will reveal that he had an unusual ability to exploit the descriptive power of language to appeal to the senses and evoke emotional responses. Not only does he use extraordinarily vivid visual imagery, but he is equally creative with aural imagery, or the sound effects of language.

A *Vanity Fair* cartoon of Tennyson as Poet Laureate, published in July 1871

Activity

Look at these lines from the first stanza of the poem *Mariana*:

With blackest moss the flower-plots
    Were thickly crusted, one and all:
The rusted nails fell from the knots
    That held the pear to the gable-wall.
The broken sheds look'd sad and strange:
    Unlifted was the clinking latch;
    Weeded and worn the ancient thatch
Upon the lonely moated grange.

(lines 1–8)

- What is your response to these lines? What emotions do they suggest?
- How has Tennyson used language and poetic techniques effectively to make this description vivid?

Discussion

You may have responded to this description in various ways. For example, perhaps you noted feelings of sadness, loneliness and emptiness, a sense of decay and neglect, or of a place somehow frozen in time.

Tennyson has chosen his words very carefully here, both for their visual impact and for their sound qualities. Here are some examples.

- The moss is not just 'black' but *blackest*. The superlative makes the effect very intense: the moss is as black as it can possibly be.
- Words like *rusted*, *broken*, *Weeded* and *worn* build the picture of decay and neglect.
- Sound effects such as alliteration, assonance and internal rhyme are used liberally, further intensifying the power of the description. For example, the hard 'c' or 'ck' and 'st' consonants in *blackest*, *thickly crusted* – (echoed by *rusted*) – when spoken aloud create a grinding or jarring sound; no *flower* could grow in this harsh-sounding environment. The assonance on the long vowels in *lonely moated* creates a moaning sound that enhances the sense of isolation.

- The word *clinking* is onomatopoeic, echoing the sound of the latch lifting and falling back as the door shifts in the wind, but the negative *Unlifted* emphasizes what is *not* happening, and draws attention to the fact that no one comes to this lonely place.

'Variety of lyrical measures': Form and metre

Nowadays, poets are less likely to use highly formal stanzas with strictly patterned rhyme and rhythm, but to many Victorian poets these things were very important. The Romantic poets had abandoned the heroic couplets typical of the eighteenth century, and revived older forms such as the sonnet and blank verse, but in Tennyson's time this gave way to all sorts of experiments. These included using forms popular in other countries or cultures, writing in dialect, or creating complex patterns with rhyme, rhythm and metre.

Newly developed technology for measuring sound was used in the scientific study of music and poetry, and theorists wrote about the psychology of the pleasurable effects poetry had on readers. In an 'Essay on English Metrical Law' published in 1857, the poet Coventry Patmore suggested that we have an 'imaginary ictus', a pulse in our minds, which likes to 'beat time' to the regular patterns of poetry as we read. The body responds too, with tapping fingers or toes, and the rhythm of poetry is said to echo the heartbeat. Try reading this line from *The Lotos-Eaters* (36) aloud:

˘ / ˘ / ˘ / ˘ / ˘ / ˘ /
And mu /sic in / his ears / his bea / ting heart / did make.

The sound of his poems was very important to Tennyson and he was very particular about how they should be read aloud – in fact, he liked to perform his poems himself and did not trust anyone else to do this properly. However, it can be helpful to read his work aloud, if only to yourself, in order to hear the aural imagery and the musical and rhythmic effects of his verse. If you can, listen to the recording of him reading *The Charge of the Light Brigade* made by Thomas Edison in 1890 (see page 82).

Tennyson was one of the most prolific of experimenters. As well as using traditional forms such as iambic pentameter blank verse, he revived old forms including unusual rhythm patterns from Ancient Greek and Latin poetry, and the Spenserian stanza that he uses in *The Lotos-Eaters*. He also created many new varieties of 'measures' of his own. Examples are the stanza forms he used for *Mariana* and *Choric Song*.

It is useful to be able to identify the metre and rhyme patterns in his poetry. If you have not already studied poetry in this way, you might find it helpful to read about it in, for example, *Exploring Literature* (by Steven Croft and Helen Cross, Oxford University Press), or online. Useful introductions can be found by searching for 'metre rhyme scansion introduction', such as http://poetryhandbookintro.blogspot.co.uk/p/basics-scansion-meter-and-rhyme.html

Of course, it is necessary to go beyond merely identifying technical features and to think about *why* Tennyson has chosen to use particular forms or patterns of rhyme and rhythm. What effects are created, and how do these help to express ideas and interrelate with the meaning of the poems? Sometimes effects are created by the use of a regular pattern or form; at other times, what is most striking is the way a rhythmic pattern is disturbed or disrupted, causing emphasis to fall in unexpected ways.

Activity

Read these lines from stanza 1 of *The Lotos-Eaters*:

'Courage!' he said, and pointed toward the land,
'This mounting wave will roll us shoreward soon.'
In the afternoon they came unto a land
In which it seemed always afternoon.
All round the coast the languid air did swoon,
Breathing like one that hath a weary dream.
Full-faced above the valley stood the moon;
And like a downward smoke, the slender stream
Along the cliff to fall and pause and fall did seem.

(lines 1–9)

93

- What rhythmic patterns are used in these lines? Which lines seem regular and which lines seem to disrupt the expected rhythm?
- How has Tennyson used these rhythms to enhance the effectiveness of his description?

Discussion

In *The Lotos-Eaters* Tennyson uses a particular form known as the Spenserian stanza (see Notes page 62), which is made up of eight lines of iambic pentameter with alternate lines rhyming, rounded off with a single alexandrine – a line with six iambic feet (and therefore six stressed beats) rather than five. In keeping with the description of the sleepy, languid landscape and atmosphere, the regular iambic metre in lines 5–8 creates a gentle, rocking rhythm, and with the stress falling on the final syllable, each line seems to come to rest, slowing down the movement and adding to the sense of inertia.

In two places, the rhythm differs significantly from this pattern. In the opening line, the first syllable is stressed, and the shout of *'Courage!'* stands out commandingly. This catches the attention of the reader as well as that of the sailors to whom it is addressed. The final alexandrine also disturbs the expected pattern, but in a different way. The extra foot seems to slow down or stop time, underlining exactly what the words portray: as it appears *to fall and pause and fall*, the waterfall seems momentarily suspended in space.

In 'Now sleeps the crimson petal', Tennyson uses the form of the *ghazal*, an ancient Persian or Indian love poem that is composed according to certain rules:

- it is made up of couplets, with the same rhythmic pattern in each line
- every few lines, the same word appears at the end of the line, to create a form of rhyme
- certain symbolic images are included: roses, lilies, cypress trees, peacocks, stars.

Activity

Identify the above features in *'Now sleeps the crimson petal'*. What effects has Tennyson achieved using this clearly defined form?

Discussion

You will see that the poem follows the form closely. The lines all have 10 syllables, the central part of the poem is arranged in couplets, and the word 'me' is repeated at intervals, to create rhyme. The prescribed images are used, but not rigidly; they sound natural and appropriate, not contrived.

This is perhaps the most sensual and erotic love poem Tennyson ever wrote. (In *The Princess*, Princess Ida reads it to the injured prince when she is nursing him. He is half asleep, but 'Fill'd thro' and thro' with Love'.)

It is a beautiful evocation of nightfall in a garden, as the flowers close up and stillness descends. The repetition of *Now* creates the sense of an acute, moment-by-moment awareness of each small change in the surroundings. In lines 2–3, the negative *Nor* intensifies the sense of hushed stillness, as if the movements of the *cypress* and goldfish are expected, but absent. Tiny patterns of repeated sounds enhance the effect, for example the assonance in *winks* and *fin*, and the alliteration in *fin* and *porphyry font*, suggest the delicate movements of the invisible goldfish. The imagery is sensual, inviting in a tender, loving way. As the flowers close, the lovers become 'open' to each other and she invites him to *be lost in me*.

Themes

The artist's dilemma

Matthew Arnold wrote:

> Ah! Two desires toss about
> The poet's feverish blood.

One drives him to the world without,
And one to solitude.
 (*Stanzas in Memory of the Author of 'Obermann'*, lines 93–96)

What does it mean to be an artist, and how does it affect the way someone lives? Tennyson knew he wanted to be a poet from a very young age, and he held to this purpose throughout his life. He never held down a job, or 'worked' in the ordinary sense, although sometimes his friends and critics suggested he might be the better for doing so. He managed, eventually, to earn a very good income from his poetry, something no poet has much hope of doing today. However, a full-time artist or writer is continually under pressure to find the inspiration to keep producing good work. Sometimes this requires long periods of solitary reflection and concentration, even isolation, yet there is also a human need to be in contact with others. In Tennyson's time, Victorian values demanded active participation in the world, hard work and a strong sense of civic duty and responsibility.

Tennyson struggled with these conflicting demands, while his family troubles and his susceptibility to depression (see page 11) added to his sense that engagement in life might be more trouble than it was worth. Despite his great capacity for friendship and his love for the natural world, this sometimes led him to withdraw from relationships and to feelings of ambivalence about life itself. These dilemmas are explored indirectly in several of his poems.

In *Mariana*, the themes of isolation and abandonment, and the idea of death as a release from struggle, are pervasive. The critic Harold Bloom has raised the possibility that Mariana might be addicted to her state of unfulfilled longing. He considers the poem 'deliciously unhealthy', and suggests she is 'too happy in [her] unhappiness to want anything more… She doesn't want or need the other who *cometh not*. What would she do with him?'

The Lady of Shalott can also be seen as a myth representing the conflict between two opposite desires: to be fully involved in life, with all its excitement, love and pain, or to stay outside the action and just observe it; 'the wish not to face reality and the wish to face it' (Christopher Ricks, *Tennyson*, see Further Reading page 147). The Lady of Shalott is an artist, so she must live at a distance from the 'real' world, which she can only observe, indirectly, as *shadows* in her mirror. Her constant weaving, echoed in the rhyme and rhythm patterns of the poem, seems to keep her safe and reasonably cheerful. Tennyson, from his boyhood, found relief from pressure and unhappiness in 'weaving' his poetry; he suggested later in *In Memoriam* (V, page 41) that the production of *measured language* (6) was a drug that numbed his pain and offered protection from the world.

Tennyson's son Hallam, in *Alfred, Lord Tennyson: A Memoir* (see Further Reading), suggests that the 'key' to *The Lady of Shalott* is to be found in Part II, lines 69–72, when the lady sees *two young lovers lately wed* and admits to being *half sick of shadows*. He says this has 'deep human significance'. At this point, she recognizes what is lacking in her own life, and when Lancelot appears – not shadowy, but blazing with life – she decides to escape her isolation. But this escape kills her.

Perhaps the most powerful exploration of this dilemma appears in *The Lotos-Eaters*, and particularly in the *Choric Song* of the addicted sailors.

Activity

Remind yourself of *The Lotos-Eaters* (page 28) and *Choric Song* (page 29).

Focusing on *Choric Song*:
- What arguments do the addicted mariners use for remaining in the land of the Lotos-eaters?
- What arguments or evidence *against* addiction can you find in the poem?
- Which side do you feel makes the stronger case?

Discussion

The mariners focus alternately on the attractions of the land of the Lotos-eaters and their discontent with their ordinary lives.

- They speak of the beautiful sights and sounds offered by what seems an attractive natural landscape, with *night-dews on still waters* (48), *blissful skies* (52), *crisping ripples on the beach,/ And tender curving lines of creamy spray* (106–107) and gentle soothing music.

- In stanza II they complain about the harshness of their life of *wanderings* at sea, and about the endless *toil*, *heaviness* and *sharp distress* of human life.

- Nature's cycles happen without effort; *Sun-steep'd* and *dew-fed* (74–75), the leaf has all its needs catered for without effort. Why should human beings, supposedly at the top of the evolutionary tree, *the roof and crown of things* (69), be forced to labour endlessly, when all other beings are allowed to rest?

- It is pointless to engage in life, since life ends in death anyway (86). They might as well just give up and drift towards *dark death* – it's so much more restful (98).

- They want to live in a sweet *half-dream* (101) of the past. Their memories of their families are *Dear* (114), but they have been away so long that they have convinced themselves they will no longer be missed or wanted, and that their presence would only be disturbing if they returned.

- There may be conflict at home, but they feel impotent to deal with it or *settle order once again* (127). Since the gods control things anyway, it is easier not to bother; there is no point in trying to *war with evil* (94).

- Even death is preferable to living on into old age, facing *Trouble on trouble, pain on pain,/ Long labour* (129–130) and seeing no joy ahead.

- The lotos gives them a false sense of power, enabling them to feel *like Gods* (155) who live on another plane, above all the overwhelming list of dangers – *Blight and famine, plague and earthquake* (160) – that threaten human life, and the useless *enduring toil* (166) that leads only to suffering and death.

- Even religion would offer no comfort – the gods are *careless of mankind* (155) and only *smile* and find *little meaning* in the *lamentation* of humans (162–164).

Arguments against addiction are more subtle, and appear in the vocabulary used to describe the landscape, and through the way the mariners present themselves.

- Throughout, although lotos-land is, on the face of it, very beautiful, the vocabulary often hints at an underlying sense of decay and unhappiness. In *The Lotos-Eaters*, the idea of a land where it is *always afternoon* (4) suggests the cloying quality of a place that seems stuck near the end of a day and also near the end of life. In *Choric Song* the roses are *blown* (47), the leaves *turning yellow* (75) and the apple *over-mellow* (78).

- Yellow colours, in Tennyson's poetry, often suggest something unhealthy. Here, there is amber light (102) and the *Lotos-dust* itself is *yellow* (149). Some of the other colours seem artificially bright, such as the *purple hill* (138) and *emerald-colour'd water* (141).

- The lotos is easily available, but the *peak* where it blooms is *barren*, the *cave* is *hollow* and the *alley* is *lone* (145–148).

- Although their arguments are in many ways quite compelling, the mariners themselves do not seem altogether likeable. In places, they sound unattractively self-pitying. Eventually, their repeated claims of unfairness – *Why should we only toil?* (69) – seem to take on a whining tone.

- They begin to seem lazy and their wish to abdicate responsibility, to give up the struggle to *war with evil* (94) and try to make the world a better place, is not admirable. In Victorian times, when doing one's duty in the world, accepting responsibility and stoically facing hardship were highly valued, this would have appeared more obviously reprehensible.

- They have lost their faith in the meaning of life, feeling that the gods do not care. Victorians struggled with religious doubt as though it were a sign of weakness.

- They do not sound happy, just calm and distant. They want to live in the past, brooding on their memories, in *mild-minded melancholy* (109), and there is a coldness in their detached description of their dead parents as *Two handfuls of white dust* (113). Even their apparently fond memories of their wives, of *their warm tears* (116), are dismissed with an excuse.

Tennyson had strong feelings about addiction – his father's alcoholism and his brother's addiction to opium caused many problems for his family. He himself was a heavy tobacco-smoker all his life, despite many attempts to give up. (See also the quotation from his letter to a friend, on page 63.) His intention was, probably, to indicate the dangers of addiction. Overall, however, the poem is a powerful portrayal of ambivalence about engagement with life, questioning the meaning and value of human action, and even of life itself.

Poetry and politics

Robert Martin, in *Tennyson: The Unquiet Heart* (see Further Reading) writes that 'Tennyson was not a political animal, but his imagination was stirred by heroism' (page 164).

Tennyson was never very much involved in the political life of his day. At times, his friends tried to prompt him to write more directly about current issues, but he was usually more at ease with the past than the present, and with exploring personal experience rather than public matters. However, he was not a recluse. He had many friends, was often at the centre of literary life in London, and he travelled a great deal, both in Britain – he was one of the first passengers on the new Liverpool and Manchester Railway in 1830 – and in Europe. He had a strong sense of social justice and admired those who took a stand against tyranny and inequality. When he and Arthur Hallam travelled to the Pyrenees in 1830, it was partly to undertake a secret mission, carrying money and despatches in invisible ink to Spanish revolutionaries whose cause had become popular with the idealistic young men at Cambridge. He also composed a sonnet on hearing news of the Polish uprising against Russian domination in 1831:

> How long, O God, shall men be ridden down,
> And trampled under by the last and least
> Of men?
>
> (*Poland*, lines 1–3)

And, of course, he was later moved by the impressive but futile heroism at the Battle of Balaclava, during the Crimean War, which led him to compose *The Charge of the Light Brigade* in 1854.

On a more personal level, he had a hatred of snobbery and a profound distaste for 'Mammonism'– the obsession with money – which he saw as poisoning society with financial inequality and aggressive consumerism, although his own relationship to money and social position was complex. He vented his strong feelings on such matters in *Maud*, which begins with an angry tirade in which the protagonist suggests that even war would be better than a so-called peace in which 'the poor are hovell'd and hustled together, each sex, like swine,/ When only the ledger lives' (34–35) – the 'ledger' being the financial accounts book – and when 'A Mammonite mother kills her babe for a burial fee' (45).

Perhaps, too, this is why he was inspired to re-tell the story of *Godiva*, in which the heroine stands up against her husband's cruelty and snobbish dismissal of the people of Coventry:

> She told him of their tears,
> And pray'd him, 'If they pay this tax, they starve.'
> Whereat he stared, replying, half-amazed,
> 'You would not let your little finger ache
> For such as *these*?' – 'But I would die,' said she.
>
> (lines 19–23)

The narrator comments that not only the 'new men' of his day, *we, that prate / Of rights and wrongs, have loved the people well, / And loathed to see them overtax'd* (lines 7–9).

Women in society

Godiva is quite unusual among Tennyson's 'heroines', for some of them do not seem very heroic at all. In his earlier poems, women are either represented as merely superficial 'pretty' portraits – his friend Edward FitzGerald referred to them as 'a stupid Gallery of Beauties' – or seem to fit the stereotype of the Victorian woman as a rather helpless, childlike creature.

In the first half of the nineteenth century, it was still a common belief that it was 'natural' for men and women to have very different roles in society. Men were expected to dominate public life and to work in the institutions of government, business and academia. Women, seen as weaker and more emotional, were to be protected and were expected to fulfil their 'natural' purpose as mothers and homemakers.

However, as the century went on, gender roles were questioned more and more, and the issue of women's rights grew in importance. Writers and poets contributed to the debate. For example, Elizabeth Barrett Browning made a strong case for women's equality in her verse novel *Aurora Leigh* (1857).

In his long poem *The Princess*, which grew out of a discussion with Emily Sellwood, who later became his wife, Tennyson tackled the question of women's education. For women nowadays, the message of the poem is confused and the conclusion is not very satisfactory. The women's university he invents is a stereotyped and at times rather ridiculous fantasy in which beautiful girls drift around in colourful robes that set off the different shades of their hair, while their lectures and studies are presented very superficially. At the end of the poem, the freethinking princess changes her priorities, chooses to conform to the traditional role, and marries the prince. However, although the result may seem counter-productive, he was one of the first writers to give substantial attention to the subject, and was perhaps somewhat ahead of his time.

Activity

Compare the ways Tennyson presents women in *Mariana*, *The Lady of Shalott*, and *Godiva*.

Discussion

In some respects Mariana is hardly there in the poem, as a person, at all. Her appearance is never described and the only direct evidence of her voice lies in the refrain, in which we hear her repeatedly declaiming her misery, that her *life is dreary* and that she is *aweary*. At the same time, the poem is full of her; every detail it describes, of the landscape and of her surroundings, seems saturated with her emotions. In this way, it portrays the idea of utter paralysis; Mariana is forever helpless and without hope, incapable of changing anything by herself.

The Lady of Shalott has perhaps a more substantial presence. Her world is also one of *shadows* (71), but unlike Mariana she seems at first to be self-reliant and not unhappy. However, when she tries to take an active part in the world and makes her decisive move towards fulfilment – which could be seen as a courageous step – she is instantly punished. There is no physical description of her until the final section of the poem, and by then her fate is sealed. She lies in her boat *robed in snowy white* (136). The image is one of helpless femininity.

Godiva, whose heroism attracted Tennyson, is very different, although the male and female characters in the story are presented rather stereotypically. She shows the traditionally 'feminine' virtues of empathy and compassion, but she also has strong beliefs, is courageous and determined, and acts decisively. She stands against her *grim* (12) and masculine husband with his – somewhat cartoon-like – aggressive and ostentatious appearance, *His beard a foot before him and his hair / A yard behind* (18–19).

However, it has been suggested that Tennyson pays too much attention, on this occasion, to his heroine's appearance, and that his description of her – as she undresses, *looking like a summer moon / Half-dipt in cloud* (45–46), and lets down her hair – is rather erotic, and therefore not sufficiently respectful of her achievement. The critic Leigh Hunt wrote:

> the ticklishness of the position of Lady Godiva is exceedingly well characterised… But the true spirit… is not hit in this treatment of the subject. The Feelings of the heroine's heart ought to have been more spoken of, and those of the good people inside the houses, who did not think of 'peeping', like the rascally tailor, but wept, and prayed, and loved the unseen angel that was going along. This would have been the way to do honour to the glorious Coventry heroine.

John Collier's *Lady Godiva* was painted in about 1898

Love and loss

Love and friendship were a powerful influence in Tennyson's life and work, but a great deal of his writing was prompted not by romance or happiness, but by the loss of love, through separation or bereavement.

Even in his earlier work, love is rarely a joyful affair. *Mariana* freezes a young woman in an unending state of despair as she yearns for the lover who has deserted her, while *The Lady of Shalott* is condemned to die when she tries to leave her isolation and reach out for love. Only *The Princess* brings a love story to a happy ending, and there the outcome is unsatisfactory for other reasons (see page 102), while in *Maud* love leads to violence, death and madness.

The death of Arthur Hallam in 1833 had a profound effect on Tennyson for many years and was probably the single most influential event in his life. Even marriage and the birth of his children did not affect him so deeply. It prompted the writing of the greatest and most enduringly popular of his works. The sense of loss pervades poems such as *Ulysses* and *Tithonus*, but there it is handled obliquely; in other poems, such as '*Break, break, break*', he writes about it more directly. But it is in *In Memoriam A.H.H.*, dedicated to the memory of Hallam and generally considered to be Tennyson's masterpiece, that his grief is explored in the fullest and most personal way.

Written over the course of 17 years, *In Memoriam* charts the long process of coming to terms with bereavement. Although the 133 lyrics of which it is composed are clearly related to different phases in his own suffering and gradual recovery, according to his son he wanted the work to be thought of as 'a poem, not an actual biography... "I" is not always the author speaking of himself, but the voice of the human race speaking through him' (Hallam Tennyson, *Alfred, Lord Tennyson: A Memoir*, Volume I, page 305).

Perhaps this is why a poem on a subject that might seem morbid became so overwhelmingly popular. Within *In Memoriam*, Tennyson confronts some of the great questions of his time. Can you hold onto religious faith in the face of new scientific discoveries and theories that seem to deny the existence of God? How do you come to terms with death if you can no longer be certain of Christian beliefs, with their promise of immortality?

Above all, it offered readers something new from poetry, by speaking in a direct, personal way about experiences all people will share. The poem has helped many to come to terms with the loss of a loved one by reminding them that they are not alone and that their feelings are part of the universal experience of being human. Queen Victoria, who read the poem after the death of her husband Prince Albert, wrote that after the Bible, *In Memoriam* was the greatest comfort to her in her grief.

The poem as a whole shows grieving to be a journey with progress and setbacks, but with a gradual movement towards healing and a new life. More recently, people who work with the bereaved have given names to different stages in the process of grieving. For example, they can be described as:

1 Shock, numbness and feelings of unreality
2 Disbelief, longing, and searching for the dead person
3 Anxiety, anger or guilt
4 Remembering
5 Depression and loss of faith
6 Acceptance and healing

Activity

All of these stages of bereavement can be found in *In Memoriam*. Can you identify some of these in the selection of poems on pages 41–46?

Discussion

V: Shock and numbness. He is almost too shocked to express his feelings, but finds writing poetry helps to numb his pain.

VII: Disbelief, yearning, and searching. Yearning for contact with his friend, he goes to his house, unable fully to take in that he is dead.

XXIV: Yearning and remembering. The past seems so much more attractive than the present, although he questions whether it was really so.

L: Anxiety and loss of faith. He also yearns for his friend's presence when he feels most fearful.

LXVII: There are some signs of acceptance as he imagines Hallam's grave and feels connected to him by the moonlight.

CVI and CXV: Acceptance and healing. His sadness and regret have been transformed into hope for the future, and loving memory.

The separate lyrics that make up *In Memoriam* are united not just by the over-arching theme, but by the use of a common stanza form. It is a clear, simple structure of four lines of iambic tetrameter, but the slightly unusual *abba* rhyme scheme creates a subtly circular effect. While the ideas in the poems move forward, the rhyme keeps doubling back on itself, perhaps echoing the difficulty of moving forward through grief. Within this framework, each short poem uses language effectively to capture a different 'mood of sorrow'.

Activity

Read *In Memoriam* VII on page 42. What mood is evoked here, and how has Tennyson used language to articulate his feelings effectively?

Discussion

This harrowing poem captures one of the most painful experiences of grieving and creates an atmosphere of utter desolation. In the *earliest morning* (8), unable to sleep, the poet is drawn to visit the house where his dead friend had lived. The house is *Dark* (1), and alliteration emphasizes the dreariness of the *long unlovely street* (2). The negative *unlovely* also perhaps hints at a feeling of being 'unloved'.

Remembering the excitement he used to feel, his heart beating *So quickly* (4) as he waited to be welcomed, makes the absence all the harder to bear. In the same line, the phrase *waiting for a hand* is left hanging until the next stanza, suggesting that he still, as before, waits for the *hand that can be clasp'd no more*.

Activity

Read *'Break, break, break'* (page 39). How does Tennyson use the landscape to express the sense of loss?

Discussion

Compare your response with this account written by Richard Holt Hutton in 1888:

> Observe how the wash of the sea on the cold gray stones is used to prepare the mind for the feeling of helplessness with which the deeper emotions break against the hard and rigid

element of human speech; how the picture is then widened out till you see the bay with children laughing on its shore, and the sailor-boy singing on its surface, and the stately ships passing on in the offing to their unseen haven, all with the view of helping us to feel the contrast between the satisfied and the unsatisfied yearnings of the human heart. Tennyson, like every true poet, has the strongest feeling of the spiritual and almost mystic character of the associations attaching to the distant sail which takes the ship on its lonely journey to an invisible port, and has more than once used it to lift the mind into the attitude of hope or trust. But then the song returns again to the helpless breaking of the sea at the foot of crags it cannot climb, not this time to express the inadequacy of human speech to express human yearnings, but the defeat of those very yearnings themselves. Thus does Lord Tennyson turn an ordinary sea-shore landscape into a means of finding a voice indescribably sweet for the dumb spirit of human loss.

Richard Holt Hutton, 'Tennyson', *Literary Essays* (1888),
pages 361–436

Faith and doubt

Commenting on *In Memoriam* later in his life, Tennyson spoke of his 'conviction that fear, doubt and suffering will find answer and relief only through Faith in a God of Love' (Hallam Tennyson, *Memoir* Volume I, page 305).

However, this kind of religious certainty was not always available to him in his life. While many Victorians valued the Christian faith highly, and wanted to believe, doubt had crept in, making the old unquestioning faith impossible. As John Stuart Mill put it, 'To know that a feeling would make me happy if I had it, did not give me the feeling'.

Although towards the end of his life Tennyson reached something of the calm acceptance he expresses in *Crossing the Bar*, he was often subject to doubt and questioning. He was well-read, and was familiar with geology and theories of evolution even before Charles Darwin's ideas on this had become widely known.

Such knowledge called into question not just the biblical account of the creation, but also the very existence of a benevolent and loving God. Theories about evolution and 'the survival of the fittest' set religion and nature against each other. In *In Memoriam* LV, Tennyson asks:

> Are God and Nature then at strife,
>   That Nature lends such evil dreams?
>   So careful of the type she seems,
> So careless of the single life

Religion teaches that God cares for every individual soul, and promises eternal life; nature says that every individual must die and that only species need to be kept going. But in the next poem, LVI, Tennyson questions even this. On the grand scale of evolution, observable through geology, even species or 'types' are of no importance. Nature, 'red in tooth and claw', 'cries, "A thousand types are gone: / I care for nothing, all shall go'."

With the traditional foundations for faith and a sense of meaning so thoroughly undermined, even human existence could seem terrifyingly pointless. The mariners in *The Lotos-Eaters* and *Choric Song* use this as one of the justifications for their choice to escape into addiction rather than face the seemingly meaningless *toil* of human life.

Activity

Read *In Memoriam* L (page 43). How does Tennyson present ideas about religious faith and doubt here?

Discussion

The poem resembles a prayer, but with the repeated *Be near me* addressed not to God, but to Tennyson's dead friend, suggesting a belief, at this point, that the dead continue to exist, as souls or spirits. However, what the poem presents more strongly is the pain of depression and doubt, and the terror of meaninglessness.

Stanza 1 describes vividly the physical experience of anxiety and depression. The outer lines suggest the *slow* lethargy of a *low* mood, with softer consonants and longer vowels, while the inner lines are nervous and irritable, with broken rhythms and the short, sharp rhyme of *prick / tingle... sick*. The repetition of *And* suggests how overwhelmed he is by all these symptoms of fear and despair.

In stanzas 2–3, his *trust* and *faith* are *conquer*ed by his pain. From this perspective, life appears meaningless and destructive. As in the references to evolution discussed above, all forms of life are mere *dust* to be scattered randomly by *Time*, which is a *maniac*. (Contrast the religious idea that God's actions are benign and meaningful.) The metaphors are even more disturbing in stanza 3, where people are compared to short-lived insects that *lay their eggs* to preserve the species and then *die*. What they create is *petty*; they *sting and sing* – they do harm and they do beautiful things – but none of this is meaningful. The very regular rhythm here suggests this repetitive cycle of life is merely tedious and pointless.

In stanza 4, the movement is smoother and calmer. Death, the end of *human strife*, will come as a relief. Finally, faith seems to be reinstated, as he looks forward to his friend showing him the way to *eternal day*. This is not a glorious new day, however, but only a subdued *twilight*.

Narrative and drama: Tennyson's storytelling

Starting points

Tennyson was often most successful as a storyteller when he 'borrowed' stories and characters, rather than when he invented his own from scratch. This does not mean that he was not original, however. Many other great poets – including Shakespeare, Milton and Keats – have drawn ideas from history, from mythology, or from the work of earlier writers, added a new 'spin', and made them their own.

Many of Tennyson's narratives are based on medieval legends, such as the tales of King Arthur, or on the classical texts of Ancient Greece and Rome, by poets such Homer, Virgil, or Ovid. These were familiar to him from childhood onwards, as his father gave him a thorough education in literature and classical civilization, and this gave him a rich bank of resources to draw on. Valentine Cunningham writes:

> The Greek and Roman authors Tennyson read early on stayed as friends, providing him with a large, echoing repertoire of ideas, moods, lines, tags, verse forms, stories, narrative moments, characters, models, for repeated plundering and recycling. His new poems live with parasitic zest on the old classical ones.
>
> (*Victorian Poetry Now*, 2011, page 452)

In his own time, people sometimes urged Tennyson to write on more contemporary themes, such as politics or social problems, and the critic R.H. Horne suggested that he was 'less at home with his own day than with antiquity'. However, although the stories he chose to use are often ancient, many of the ideas and issues he explores through them are both personal and universally relevant. In a sense, this makes them timeless. R.H. Horne went on to say that most of his poems 'which contain human character in a progressive story are taken from various sources; but they are taken by a master-hand, and infused with new life and beauty, new thought and emotion'.

Today, do you think readers find Tennyson's use of ancient and medieval stories off-putting, or interesting?

The dramatic monologue

In the Victorian age there was a shift in emphasis in the work of many poets, away from external, public and practical affairs and towards a concern with the inner life of the individual (see pages 3–4). A growing interest in psychology and mental health was reflected in forms of poetry that explored the inner workings of the mind. Sometimes this is straightforward introspection, where the poet examines his or her own thoughts and feelings, doubts and questionings. Tennyson writes in this way in many short lyric poems, which address the reader directly and portray his own perceptions and emotions. These usually focus on one particular moment or experience. The many poems that comprise *In Memoriam* and the songs from *The Princess* are examples of this form.

However, it was also characteristic for nineteenth-century poets to explore the workings of the mind using less direct and more dramatic approaches. In particular, the dramatic monologue became a popular form. In a dramatic monologue, the poet tells a story or presents a dramatic scene by adopting a persona or creating a character who is the sole speaker in the poem. The presence of other characters – the listener(s) or auditor(s) – is made apparent to a greater or lesser degree through the words of the speaker. These may be shadowy figures, merely implied. In some cases, the speaker might address them directly, or report and comment on their words and actions, but they never speak for themselves. This means that there are always other sides to the story, about which we can only guess and imagine.

This method of 'impersonation' allows the poet to tell a story from one person's point of view, but also to explore the character's psychological make-up, revealing different facets of personality and motivation. A special feature is that the poet can also 'undercut' the speaker in various ways. For example, the character may betray conscious or unconscious motives that conflict with what is being expressed on the surface. In other words, the speaker can 'give himself (or herself) away'. You may be familiar with some of Robert Browning's dramatic monologues, such as *My Last Duchess* or *Porphyria's Lover*, where this device is obvious: the speakers present their behaviour and feelings as normal and rational, while simultaneously revealing themselves to be insanely jealous murderers.

Alternatively, the poet can expose the speaker by choosing language that more subtly undermines the surface message. Tennyson's use of the dramatic monologue is less sensational and more personal than these examples by Browning, although the protagonist in his long dramatic poem *Maud* is volatile, extreme, and at times, insane (see Notes page 83).

An American critic, Ina Beth Sessions, defined seven features that go into the making of a dramatic monologue (in 'The Dramatic Monologue', *PMLA* 62, 1947, pages 503–516):

- speaker
- audience
- occasion
- revelation of character
- interplay between speaker and audience
- dramatic action
- action that takes place in the present.

Activity

Tithonus (page 52) is an example of a dramatic monologue. Read lines 1–10 (but do not look at the Notes just yet).
- What can you deduce about the speaker from these lines?
- What moods are created here? Compare lines 1–4 with the rest of the stanza.

Now look at the Notes to the poem, on page 86, which explain the background to the speaker's words. How does this knowledge help you make sense of this first stanza?

Discussion

You may have noted that the speaker describes himself as *A white-hair'd shadow* (8) and says that he is *slowly* withering (6), suggesting old age. When he says he is *roaming like a dream* (8), he sounds a bit unreal, or ghostlike. He also tells us that he is immortal. We might expect this to be a privilege, but the unexpected pairing of the words *cruel immortality* (5) suggests otherwise.

In lines 1–4 the usual cycles of nature, such as the seasons and the natural lifespan of *Man* or *the swan*, which lead to death and decay, are presented in language that is melancholy (the autumnal mists *weep*) but also comfortingly smooth. The rhythm is a regular, gently rocking iambic pentameter. By contrast, in line 5, the mood changes as the speaker draws attention to himself, singling himself out. With the stress on *Me only*, the rhythmic pattern is disrupted, while the unexpected, rather abrupt words *cruel* and *Consumes*, followed by the mid-line colon in line 6, bring it to a standstill.

From the Notes, you will have learned that Tithonus was a man who fell in love with a goddess – Aurora, goddess of the dawn – who granted him immortality but not eternal youth, thus sentencing him instead to an eternally increasing old age. This explains why he is *white-hair'd* and *roaming* in the *East*, where the dawn rises.

We can also see why there is a reversal of expectations. Normally it is death that *Consumes* and is thought of as *cruel*, but for Tithonus, the opposite is true: immortality is far more cruel. It is also unnatural, interrupting the regular cycles of life and death, which to him now seem soothing and desirable.

Activity

Now read the whole of *Tithonus* and think about these questions.
- How does the character Tithonus tell his story? How do we learn about the past as well as the present?
- How is the listener or auditor – Aurora – presented in the poem?
- Apart from telling the story, what message or moral point might Tennyson be making in the poem?
- How would it feel to be Aurora? How does she see the situation? Imagine being young and beautiful and married to someone very, very old. Experiment with writing a monologue of your own, in the voice of Aurora, in which she tells her side of the story. This could be in verse or prose, and could be serious or humorous.

Discussion

Tithonus tells his story by speaking directly to Aurora, reminiscing about the past and how the current situation came about. He reminds her that once he too was *glorious in his beauty* (12) and that when she chose him, she made him feel like *none other than a God* (14).

Towards the end of the poem, he looks back longingly on their youthful love-making, describing in quite erotic language how he felt his *blood / Glow* as he lay,

> Mouth, forehead, eyelids, growing dewy-warm
> With kisses balmier than half-opening buds
> Of April...

(lines 58–60)

He relates how he asked for immortality, which she readily granted, only to find it led to the torture of having to live forever as *Immortal age beside immortal youth* (22). The repetition in lines 21–22 emphasizes how painful he finds the contrast, now that all his own beauty is *in ashes* (23).

Trapped in this desperate state, he begs her to *take back thy gift* (27), but in the following stanzas we realize that she cannot help. He describes how each time he asks to be released, she cries, silently, leaving her tears *on my cheek* (45), but departs without answering. He is forced to confront the old saying that even gods and goddesses are unable to *recall their gifts* (49) or undo their actions.

Thus, his speech to Aurora reveals not only his present state and feelings, but also the history of their relationship and the past events that led to the current terrible situation.

Aurora simultaneously has the characteristics of a young woman and of the dawn, and this is reflected in the language used to describe her. There are references to the East and to the rosy colours of dawn – *redden* (37), *crimson'd* (56) – and to her light and *dewy* warmth (58) as her *eyes brighten* (38), *flakes of fire* (42) appear and her *curls kindle into sunny rings* (54).

In stanza 2, he describes her generosity in granting his request for immortality *with a smile* – but does make the point that this was the easy and unthinking generosity of someone who has so much that she can afford to be careless with her gifts, *Like wealthy men who care not how they give* (16–17). He does not seem to blame her, but does complain in strong terms that it is her *Hours* – goddesses of time – that have *marr'd and wasted* him, leaving him *maim'd* (18–20).

He reports that her eyes *fill with tears* (26) at his words. Is she sympathetic and sad for him? Does she still love him? Or is she also trapped by the relationship, and perhaps repelled by him? She does not speak, so we cannot know.

If the poem has a 'moral', it would seem to be a warning to humans not to get above themselves – not to wish for the unnatural *goal* of immortality, but to recognize the natural limits of their *kindly race* and accept that death is necessary and appropriate, or *meet for all* (29–31). To Tithonus, *men that have the power to die* are *happy*, and the dead are *happier* still (70–71).

Characterization

Robert Martin, in *Tennyson: The Unquiet Heart*, writes that Tennyson 'had a strong sense of character so long as it was his own' (page 344).

Tennyson's narrative poems and dramatic monologues are usually designed not just to tell a story, but to delve into an idea, an emotion or a question about life. In a similar way, he uses the characters in his poetry to explore some of the issues and dilemmas he was grappling with himself. For this reason, the question sometimes arises as to whether his characters stand alone as separate creations in their own right, or whether they are also containers, or outlines, into which Tennyson could project his own thoughts and feelings.

Activity

Read *The Lady of Shalott* and think about the characters of the lady herself and of Lancelot. How are they presented? To what extent do you feel they are real people?

Discussion

The poem is narrated in the third person, and in Part I the lady's mysterious presence in the tower and within the surrounding landscape is introduced from the point of view of those outside, who do not know her and have never seen her. The only sign of her existence is her song, heard only at night, which *echoes cheerly* (30): she does not sound unhappy.

In Part II, the perspective shifts to the inside of her tower, to the lady herself and to her reflected view of the outside world.

Her appearance is not described, but we are told of her actions – her endless weaving – and given some hints about her thoughts and feelings. Her lack of a *loyal knight and true* (62) could imply loneliness, but apart from the strange curse, she has *little other care* (44) and still *delights* (64) in her weaving, until the sight of *two young lovers* prompts her to admit that she is *half sick of shadows* (70–71).

The arrival of Sir Lancelot in Part III is, it seems, irresistible. Her movement towards him is decisive (lines 109–110), but instantly activates the curse. Finally, in Part IV, the viewpoint shifts back to that of the outside world. Her song, now *mournful* (145), is heard and there is the famous description of her, *robed in snowy white* (136), which is depicted in several famous pre-Raphaelite paintings. The onlookers are fearful at the sight of her corpse, and Lancelot comments on her *lovely face* (169), but she remains a shadowy figure.

Lancelot seems very different. His appearance is described in detail in Part III, and in every way he appears bright, powerful and solid. The colours are rich and bold: *golden*, *silver*, *purple* and *coal-black*; we are told his armour *flamed*, *sparkled* and *Burn'd*, and there are strong sounds and images, such as *His broad clear brow in sunlight glow'd*, which makes him sound full of life and energy. However, he too is mysterious, and rather like a vision or a painting. His words at the end suggest that although, ironically, he has no understanding of the lady's story and his role in it, he is thoughtful, and not unkind. Otherwise, we have little sense of him as a person.

There is very little to make either the lady or Lancelot into 'real' characters, but their story is a fairy tale, and fairy tales are not designed to be realistic. Characters are 'types' rather than unique individuals, and their plots work on a different, less conscious level as 'symbols of inner experience that provide insight into human behaviour' (*Oxford Companion to Fairy Tales*, 2000). It is interesting to think about how this might have contributed to the enduring popularity of this strange, magical tale.

It has also been suggested that the poem explores Tennyson's own situation as a poet, faced by conflicting desires: to be involved in the world, or to withdraw from it in order to focus on his art. For more on this, see pages 95–97.

'I am half sick of shadows', said the Lady of Shalott by John William
Waterhouse, 1915

Activity

Read *Ulysses* (page 34). What is your impression of Ulysses himself,
and how does Tennyson present him at different stages in the poem?

Discussion

Ulysses begins by expressing frustration with his own land and people
and shows a certain amount of disdain for them. He seems dismissive
of his *aged wife* (3), as if unwilling to accept that he too is old now.
The land is *barren* (2) and the people *savage* (4), and evidently he
despises their lifestyle, as he makes them sound little better than
animals that *hoard, and sleep, and feed* (5). Worst of all, they don't
know him – they don't seem to give him the recognition and respect
he feels he deserves.

As he continues, he reveals that it is his nature to be *always roaming with a hungry heart* (12). It is the intensity of the experience of adventure that is important: whether he *enjoy'd* or *suffer'd*, he did so *greatly* (7–8). He is a thrill-seeker, who delights in *battle*; he needs to be where there is action, and to be *honour'd* (15–16).

His words suggest he is energetic and demanding. To stay at home would be *dull* (22) and *vile* (28): he would feel as useless as a rusty sword, when he wants to *shine in use* (23). Many lifetimes would not be enough to satisfy his craving for new experiences, but he has only one, and of that *Little remains* (26). His determination to *drink / Life to the lees* (6–7) – to live fully and adventurously right to the end – is admirable, but his tendency to look down on people who are not like him is less attractive.

In line 33 he introduces his son, who is to take over from him as ruler of Ithaca. It is clear that they are almost polar opposites. The vocabulary used to present Telemachus – *slow prudence*, *mild*, *soft*, *useful*, *blameless*, *common*, *decent* (36–40) – suggests he is everything Ulysses is not and never wants to be. Despite his claim that Telemachus is *Well-loved* by him (35), it is hard to avoid the conclusion that Ulysses has little respect for his son's character.

In lines 44–70 he orders his mariners, with whom he *strove with Gods* and shared many adventures, to accompany him on another voyage, in the hope that *Some work of noble note* can still be achieved (52–53). However, as he looks to the future, he sounds less sure of himself and a note of melancholy creeps in. He acknowledges that they are now old, *Made weak by time and fate* (69), and that death is inevitable. In spite of his energetic command to *Push off, and sitting well in order smite / The sounding furrows* (68–69), and his determination *To strive, to seek, to find, and not to yield* (70), there is an underlying feeling of uncertainty. He avoids using any definite future tense, suggesting only what *may* happen (52, 62, 63); and when he tells his sailors *'Tis not too late to seek a newer world* (57) there is a suspicion that he is trying to convince himself, as well as them, that they are still capable of heroic deeds.

This slight sense of unease or uncertainty, and some possible reasons for it, will be explored further in the next Activity.

Writers often incorporate aspects of their own personalities and experiences when they create characters, but Tennyson may have done this more than most. He was an introspective man, very familiar with the workings of his own mind, but perhaps, as the quotation at the head of this section (page 116) suggests, he was less able to enter into the experience of people whose characteristics or ways of experiencing life were different from his own. As a result, as Robert Martin puts it, he 'wrote most convincingly of the psyche of someone like himself'; the use of characters allows him to examine his own concerns indirectly, as if from a distance, but the differences between him and his characters 'lie only on the surface' (page 264).

Thus, he may adopt the persona of an ancient Greek hero, as he does in *Ulysses*, and place him in a scenario from the *Odyssey*, but underlying this is something more personal. Tennyson wrote *Ulysses* in 1833, very soon after hearing of the death of his friend Arthur Hallam. He said of the poem that 'There is more about myself in *Ulysses*, which was written under the sense of loss and that all had gone by, but that still life must be fought out to the end'. Ulysses and his men are old and have survived many adventures, but he longs to believe that he still has a future, and exhorts them to go forward with him into further action. His words are brave and defiant, yet it has often been pointed out that the poem has a kind of paradoxical undertow of weariness and reluctance. Perhaps this is not so surprising if we think of the poem having as a subtext the dilemma that faced Tennyson himself in the aftermath of the death of Arthur Hallam: how do you carry on with the struggle of life when it is the last thing you feel like doing? On some level, Ulysses is also Tennyson himself, bereaved and depressed, struggling to pull himself up by the bootstraps and to convince himself that he must get on with life.

Activity

Look once again at *Ulysses*, particularly lines 44–70. Can you identify any lines that seem for any reason to work against or undermine the effect of Ulysses' call to action?

Discussion

You may have noticed some of these lines.

- *There gloom the dark, broad seas* (45): The ships are ready, but setting out on a voyage does not sound like an attractive proposition.
- *Death closes all: but something ere the end, / Some work of noble note, may yet be done* (51–52): The words *may* and *Some* are indefinite and there is a slightly plaintive, desperate quality to the repetition in *something... Some work*: these future deeds are unknown and perhaps he doesn't fully believe in them.
- *The long day wanes: the slow moon climbs: the deep / Moans round with many voices* (55–56): In these lines, the rhythm of the iambic pentameter is stretched, with long, slow syllables and vowel sounds; the repeated 'm' sounds are cloying; it is as if he is being pulled back rather than going forward.
- He seems resigned or even attracted to the possibility of death, *that the gulfs will wash us down*, or of meeting Achilles in *the Happy Isles* – or heaven (62–64).

Time and structure

It is interesting to consider the ways that time is handled in Tennyson's poetry. In his large-scale works, Tennyson never worked chronologically. Even those, like *Maud* or *The Princess*, which do have an over-arching storyline, were constructed from many shorter pieces, often composed at different times, so that they do not present a continuous flow. Instead, the movement from one time and place to another is used dramatically and to create contrast.

In his shorter poems, it is rare for his narratives to follow a conventional chronological line. The tale of *Godiva* is told plainly enough, but is still enclosed within a 'frame', as Tennyson begins and ends by reflecting on the story from the perspective of his own time. *The Lady of Shalott* also appears on the surface to be a straightforward piece of storytelling. Organized like a ballad, it does narrate a series of events; the lady and her setting are introduced, Sir Lancelot rides by, and she looks away from her mirror, activating the curse that must lead to her death. Yet even here, things are not straightforward. Her situation is a puzzle that provokes many questions – and these are not answered within the story. Who is she, and what exactly is the nature of the curse that has imprisoned her? How did it come about? The answers to these questions lie in the past, in a mysterious other time, which is pervasively present and has determined the events of the story, even though it lies outside its chronological limits.

A similar sense of mystery about time is created in *Mariana*.

Activity

Read *Mariana* (page 19) and think about how this poem operates in relation to time. (It would also be useful to read the Notes on page 57.)
- What is your sense of where this story, as a whole, is 'situated' in time? Is this altered by reading about the background to the story?
- How is time presented *within* the poem?

Discussion

Reading the poem by itself, you may have found it quite mysterious and hard to place as a story. The poem is very descriptive and there is a strong sense of atmosphere. We learn that there is a female character, lonely and *weary*, who is longing for a man who never arrives. But there is no narrative in the usual sense: the story seems to be without a beginning or end and there is no action.

Tennyson points to Shakespeare's play *Measure for Measure*, where Mariana plays her part in an eventful story involving betrayal, abandonment and deception, before she is finally reunited with the absent lover. However, Tennyson seems to have little interest in the events of the narrative, focusing almost entirely on her state of mind. Mariana seems just to exist, more or less frozen in time. Nothing changes or is resolved, except that her despair becomes greater and more final in the last stanza. In stanzas 1–6, *He cometh not*, which still allows the possibility that he will arrive in the future, although there is no sign of him in the present. In stanza 7, this is replaced by the resigned and definite *He will not come*.

Within the poem, there is a contradictory sense of time being at a standstill while the cycles of day and night continue to revolve. In the course of the seven stanzas, Mariana lives through *the gray-eyed morn* (31) and the *thickest dark* (18); through the rising and setting of the moon to the time she *loathed* most, the late afternoon, when the dusty, *thick-moted sunbeam* slants across the room (77–78). Each time of day or night is conjured up, with its particular sights and sounds. The shadow of the poplar, *silver-green* (41–42), shifts with the wind and the changing light; in stanza 6, *The blue-fly sung in the pane; the mouse / Behind the mouldering wainscot shriek'd*. They are trapped in the house just as Mariana is herself.

By stanza 7, the small, repetitive (and onomatopoeic) sounds of the *sparrow's chirrup*, the *slow clock ticking* and the monotonous rustle of the *poplar* have become a form of mental torture that *did all confound / Her sense*.

Do you think this illusion, of time endlessly revolving, yet simultaneously standing still, is an effective way to portray the experience of waiting?

John Everett Millais' painting *Mariana in the Moated Grange*, 1851

The sense of time is no more straightforward in the dramatic poems and monologues. In conversation, stories are likely to take shape in a piecemeal fashion as we move back and forth between memories of the past, reflections on the present and projections into the future. In a dramatic monologue, which represents a stylized conversation taking place at a particular point in time, the narrative elements are assembled in a similar way. Explanations and descriptions of what is going on in the present moment are interspersed with references to the past and future, enabling us to build up an idea of how the current situation came about and to think about how events may unfold in the future, as we saw earlier in *Tithonus* (page 113).

To explore this further, look again at *Ulysses* and the *Choric Song* of the Lotos-eaters. Identify where the speakers refer to past, present and future.

Settings

Since many of Tennyson's narrative poems are based on tales from ancient or medieval times, the settings are created to fit. For poems set in exotic places, he would carefully research the environment and plant life, but he also drew inspiration from the natural landscapes he saw around him. The flat, watery fenlands of his native Lincolnshire provide the setting for *Mariana* and are also echoed in the river scenes in *The Lady of Shalott*. He was delighted by a visit to the French Pyrenees with Arthur Hallam and incorporated the rugged mountains and high waterfalls he saw there into the island setting of *The Lotos-Eaters*.

Tennyson loved nature and observed its details closely. He was also extremely short-sighted all his life, and it is interesting to consider how this may have affected his view of the world. Small features, such as plants or flowers, which he could see easily, are described in detail in his writing. However, the long and middle distance, for him, would have appeared very blurred, and this may be mirrored in the landscapes of his poetry, which sometimes seem misty and indistinct; intense, beautiful, yet disembodied, or not located in the real world.

One of the most distinctive features of his poetry is his special ability to create settings that are, in John Stuart Mill's words, 'not mere pictures, but states of emotion, embodied in sensuous imagery'. Like Arthur Hallam, Mill recognized 'his great power of creating scenery in keeping with some state of human feeling; so fitted to it as to be the embodied symbol of it, and to summon up the state of feeling itself, with a force not to be surpassed by anything but reality'.

The presentation of aspects of nature as if they possess human feelings or characteristics is known, in literary terms, as the pathetic fallacy, and is considered a particularly typical feature of Victorian poetry. The term was coined in 1856 by the philosopher and critic John Ruskin. He suggested that 'violent feelings' cause us to see 'false impressions of external things'; in more psychological language, we project our feelings onto aspects of nature, so that the weather seems 'angry', or a primrose 'lonely', when of course they are not. Ruskin was critical of writers who over-used the device, and suggested that the best poet was:

> the man who perceives rightly in spite of his feelings, and
> to whom the primrose is for ever nothing else than itself – a
> little flower, apprehended in the very plain and leafy fact of it,
> whatever and how many soever the associations and passions
> may be, that crowd around it.

However, he did admit that 'however great a man may be, there are always some subjects which ought to throw him off his balance' and bring him 'into the inaccurate and vague state of perception, so that the language of the highest inspiration becomes broken, obscure, and wild in metaphor' ('Of the Pathetic Fallacy' in *Modern Painters*, 1856, Volume III).

Mariana is probably the poem in which Tennyson creates a landscape most powerfully saturated with feeling, but he also does this in poems such as *The Lotos-Eaters*, the lyrics from *The Princess*, and in sections from *In Memoriam* and *Maud*.

Activity

Read the extract from *Maud*, Part II no. IV, page 48. This extract is set in the city, where the protagonist is close to breakdown (see Notes page 83). How are settings presented here, and how do they reflect the speaker's state of mind?

Discussion

Two settings are contrasted in the extract: the city where the speaker is in the present, and the garden of his old home, now lost to him, which he remembers in vivid dreams. Each is associated with different episodes and states of mind.

The cityscape mirrors his horror, hatred and self-loathing in the aftermath of the duel and his killing of Maud's brother. The city is presented as hostile and damaging – it makes the speaker's *spirit reel* (20). He finds the speed and the loud noise unbearable and describes them in terms that suggest aggression. The *wheels* – presumably of machinery and vehicles – are *roaring* (22) and later there is *sullen thunder* and *tumult* (49–50). Visually, the scene is *lurid* and threatening, the *dull red ball* of the sun smouldering behind unhealthy *yellow vapours* that *choke* both him and the city (62–66). The light, which *glares and beats* (89), intimidates him too. The anguish of his lost love is exacerbated by this place full of *Hearts with no love for me* (94).

This contrasts with the natural beauty of the garden scene he remembers, when with a clear conscience he looked forward to meeting his love. There it was *silent* (6), the *morning pure and sweet* (31); the language suggests gentleness and delicacy, with the *rivulet* that *Ripples* (41–42) and the *little flower that clings* (33). Then he was able to *delight* in *early skies* (25), whereas now he faces waking to *the shuddering dawn* (52).

An illustration for *Maud* published in about 1880; the beauty of the garden scene contrasts with the horror in later parts of the poem

Endings

Godiva and *The Lady of Shalott*, which are narrated in the third person, follow a conventional narrative arc. They move through the introduction of tension, through a climax, to a definite resolution. *Godiva*, with its well-known storyline, reaches the expected satisfying outcome. The ending of *The Lady of Shalott* is more tragic and more perplexing, but still conclusive.

Mariana, *Ulysses*, *Tithonus*, and *The Lotos-Eaters* and *Choric Song* are different. All are based on pre-existing narratives that do move forward to reach resolution, but in each case, Tennyson has chosen to place the character in the middle of the story, in a state of tension, and then leave this unresolved. If we read the poems with their back stories and future outcomes in mind, we can grasp that these states are temporary: Mariana's weary waiting will eventually end happily, Tithonus will gain relief of a sort and Ulysses will extricate his mariners from their addiction to the lotos. However, it is more important to read the poems just as they stand, in which case we are left, like the characters, suspended in a state of uncertainty. Some readers find this intriguing; others have found it frustrating. Thomas Carlyle wrote:

> If Alfred Tennyson could only make that long wail, like the winter wind, about Mariana in the Moated Grange, and could not get her to throw herself into the ditch, or could not bring her another man to help her ennui, he had much better have left her alone altogether.

Think about the endings of the narrative and dramatic poems in this selection. Do you feel that they provide satisfying conclusions?

Critical views

Throughout his life, Tennyson was inordinately sensitive to what the critics wrote about his work. Like many people, even if most of a review was positive, he would remember only the critical comments, and he did not find it easy to laugh at himself or at reviews that mocked some of his less successful poems.

His earliest publications met with a mixed reception, and were not at first widely read, but Arthur Hallam wrote of them in glowing terms in his essay 'On Some of the Characteristics of Modern Poetry'. Other responses included some bitingly sarcastic, though also humorous reviews, which Tennyson found hard to forgive.

When *Poems, Chiefly Lyrical* appeared in 1830, it received mixed reviews. William Johnson Fox wrote in the *Westminster Review*:

> That these poems will have a very rapid and extensive
> popularity we do not anticipate. Their very originality will
> prevent their being generally appreciated for a time. But
> that time will come, we hope, to a not far distant end...
> Mr Tennyson has a dangerous quality in that facility of
> impersonation... by which he enters so thoroughly into the
> most strange and wayward idiosyncrasies of other men. It must
> not degrade him into a poetical harlequin. He has higher work
> to do.
>
> *Westminster Review* (January 1831), pages 210–224

Tennyson's friend Arthur Hallam wrote in *The Englishman's Magazine* comparing him to Keats and Shelley, who:

> are both poets of sensation rather than reflection. Susceptible
> of the slightest impulse from external nature, their fine
> organs trembled into emotion at colours, and sounds,
> and movements, unperceived or unregarded by duller
> temperaments...
>   Mr Tennyson belongs decidedly to the class we have already
> described as Poets of Sensation. He sees all the forms of nature
> with the *'eruditus oculus'* [learned eye], and his ear has a
> fairy fineness. There is a strange earnestness in his worship of
> beauty, which throws a charm over his impassioned song, more
> easily felt than described, and not to be escaped by those who
> have once felt it.
>
> *The Englishman's Magazine* (August 1831), pages 616–628

On the other hand 'Christopher North' (John Wilson) in *Blackwood's Edinburgh Magazine* was scathing:

> he must consider that all the fancies that fleet across the
> imagination, like shadows on the grass or the tree-tops, are
> not entitled to be made small separate poems of – about the
> length of one's little finger; that many, nay, most of them,

should be suffered to pass away with a silent 'God bless ye',
like butterflies, single or in shoals... yet not one in a thousand
is worth being caught and pinned down on paper into
poetry...

Now, Mr Tennyson does not seem to know this; or if he do,
he is self-willed and perverse in his sometimes almost infantile
vanity... and thinks that any Thought or Feeling or Fancy that has
had the honour and the happiness to pass through *his* mind, must
by that very act be worthy of everlasting commemoration.

Blackwood's Edinburgh Magazine (May 1832), pages 721–741

Poems appeared in 1832. John Wilson Croker wrote the
following in the *Quarterly Review* about *The Lotos-Eaters*, after
quoting a passage:

Our readers will, we think, agree that this is admirably
characteristic, and that the singers of this song must have
made pretty free with the intoxicating fruit. How they got
home you must read in Homer: – Mr Tennyson – himself, we
presume, a dreamy lotus-eater, a delicious lotus-eater – leaves
them in full song.

Quarterly Review (April 1833), pages 81–96

By 1835, his work was becoming more widely known. John
Stuart Mill, who was beginning to question utilitarian views,
wrote admiringly of Tennyson's work. On *Mariana*, he wrote:

The humblest poet, who is a poet at all, could make more
than is here made of the situation of a maiden abandoned
by her lover. But that was not Mr Tennyson's idea. The
love-story is secondary in his mind. The words 'he cometh
not' are almost the only words which allude to it at all. To
place ourselves at the right point of view, we must drop
the conception of Shakespeare's Mariana, and retain only
that of a 'moated grange', and a solitary dweller within it,
forgotten by mankind. And now see whether poetic imagery
ever conveyed a more intense conception of such a place, or
the feelings of such an inmate. From the very first line, the

rust of age and the solitude of desertion are on the whole picture. Words surely never excited a more vivid feeling of physical and spiritual dreariness: and not dreariness alone – for that might be felt under many other circumstances of solitude – but the dreariness which speaks not merely of being far from human converse and sympathy, but of being *deserted* by it.

London Review (July 1835), pages 402–424

On *The Lady of Shalott*, Mill had this to say:

there is a class of readers... who read a poem with the critical understanding first, and only when they are convinced that it is right to be delighted, are willing to give their spontaneous feelings fair play... For the benefit of such readers, we tell them beforehand, that this is a tale of enchantment; and that they will never enter into the spirit of it unless they surrender their imagination to the guidance of the poet with the same easy credulity with which they would read the Arabian Nights, or, what this story more resembles, the tales of magic of the middle ages.

With *In Memoriam*, in 1850, Tennyson achieved enormous and almost unanimous popularity. Reviewing the collection, Charles Kingsley wrote that it was:

a collection of poems on a vast variety of subjects, but all united, as their name implies, to the memory of a departed friend. We know not whether to envy more – the poet the object of his admiration, or that object the monument which has been consecrated to his nobleness. For in this latest and highest volume, written at various intervals during a long series of years, all the poet's peculiar excellencies, with all that he has acquired from others, seem to have been fused down into a perfect unity, and brought to bear on his subject with that care and finish which only a labour of love can inspire...

In every place where in old days they had met and conversed; in every dark wrestling of the spirit with the doubts and fears of manhood, throughout the whole outward universe of nature, and the whole inward universe of spirit, the soul of his dead friend broods – at first a memory shrouded in blank despair, then a living presence, a ministering spirit, answering doubts, calming fears, stirring up noble aspirations, utter humility, leading the poet upward, step by step, to faith, and peace, and hope.
Fraser's Magazine (September 1850), pages 245–255

With *Maud* it was a different matter. Some readers found it brilliant, exciting and moving, but others thought it was morbid and disturbing. The conclusion, which has the protagonist leaving to fight in the Crimean War, was considered bloodthirsty, and above all, opinion was divided on the 'mad' scenes. Robert James Mann wrote in *An Explanatory Essay*:

One member of the fraternity [of critics] immediately pronounced the poem to be *a spasm*; another acutely discovered that it was a careless, visionary, and unreal *allegory of the Russian war*; a third could not quite make up his mind whether the adjective *mud* or *mad* would best apply to the work...
Tennyson's Maud Vindicated: An Explanatory Essay (1856)

George Brimley, in 'Alfred Tennyson's Poems', considered that:

English literature has nothing more dramatically expressive of a mind on the verge of overthrow, than the verses in which the shell on the Brittany coast serves as text; nothing that presents the incipient stage of madness, springing from the wrecked affections, with more of reality and pathos than the poem, 'O! That 'twere possible'... set as a jewel amid jewels; nothing that surpasses in truth and terrible force the madhouse soliloquy, 'Dead, long dead!'
'Alfred Tennyson's Poems', *Cambridge Essays* (1855)

But William Ewart Gladstone was less impressed:

The insanity expresses itself in the ravings of the homicide lover, who even imagines himself among the dead, in a clamour and confusion closely resembling an ill-regulated Bedlam, but which, if the description be a faithful one, would for ever deprive the grave of its title to the epithet of silent. It may be good frenzy, but we doubt its being as good poetry.

Quarterly Review (October 1859), pages 454–485

This photograph of Tennyson was taken at the height of his fame

Tennyson remained very popular with the public for the rest of his life, although critical acclaim for his work began to wane in the later decades of the nineteenth century, as his position was challenged by younger poets and new approaches.

In the early twentieth century, the modernist poets reacted against what they saw as Victorian tendencies to be sentimental, moralistic, worthy and wordy. T.S. Eliot, in *Essays Ancient and Modern* (1936, pages 178–187) admired *In Memoriam*: 'It is not religious because of the quality of its faith, but because of the quality of its doubt. Its faith is a poor thing, but its doubt is a very intense experience.' But Eliot feared it would become a victim of changes in modern reading habits, since 'the reading of long poems is not much practised nowadays; in the age of Tennyson it appears to have been easier'. He was less complimentary about Tennyson's narrative poems, and said that 'for narrative, Tennyson had no gift at all'– he 'could not tell a story at all'. He also said that Tennyson's later work showed he had become the 'surface flatterer of his own time'.

W.H. Auden, in his introduction to *A Selection from the Poems of Alfred, Lord Tennyson* (1944) was even less complimentary: 'He had the finest ear, perhaps, of any English poet; he was also undoubtedly the stupidest; there was little about melancholia that he didn't know; there was little else that he did.'

For much of the twentieth century, Tennyson's work was regarded as beautiful, but not of great interest. Views began to change in the 1960s. The possibility that Victorian poets were writing 'double poems', through which they could cater for the needs of society while simultaneously exploring very different or even contradictory ideas, has now become key to critical views. For example Isobel Armstrong, in *Victorian Poetry: Poetry, Poetics and Politics*, has the following to say about *In Memoriam* and *Maud*:

> Their way of combining expressive writing with critique is perhaps unparalleled in the nineteenth century. Tennyson's capacity to be startling is evident in both, but the move

from *In Memoriam* and the unseen workings beneath the
earth's surface to the pathological geology of the self in
Maud in which 'secret and silent courses' work darkly in the
physiological cells and in the brain, creates a Victorian writing
of the body which is startling in the extreme. The throbbing
pulses and coercive rhythms of *Maud* live in the writing of the
next decades even when Tennyson was deemed old-fashioned
and conventional.

Victorian Poetry: Poetry, Poetics and Politics (1993), page 283

Recent times, therefore, have seen a reassessment of Victorian
poetry, and it is now recognized that Tennyson, like many of his
contemporaries, was not a staid representative of the Victorian
establishment, but rather a challenger of the conventions of his age.

Essay Questions

1 Look at stanzas 2–3 of *Mariana* (lines 13–36). Explore the ways in which Tennyson emphasizes Mariana's feelings of hopelessness here. Refer to details in the poem in your answer.

2 A critic has said that Tennyson 'must be the greatest English writer on what it is like to be stuck in a rut' (Seamus Perry, *London Review of Books*, 20 January 2011). How far do you agree with this view? In your answer you should **either** refer to **two** or **three** poems in detail **or** range more widely through the whole selection.

3 (a) How does Tennyson tell the story in *Ulysses*?
   (b) How far would you agree with the view that Tennyson's poems reveal a deep fear of old age?

4 How does Tennyson convey the feelings of restlessness and frustration felt by Ulysses in lines 1–32 of *Ulysses*? Refer to details in the poem in your answer.

5 How far would you agree with the view that death is always presented as a welcome release in Tennyson's poetry? In your answer you should **either** refer to **two** or **three** poems in detail **or** range more widely through the whole selection.

6 (a) Write about the ways Tennyson tells the story in *Mariana*.
   (b) What do you think is significant about settings in Tennyson's poetry?

7 How does Tennyson make the characters and their actions vivid in Part III of *The Lady of Shalott* (lines 73–117)? Refer to details in the poem in your answer.

8 How does Tennyson create a sense of atmosphere in *In Memoriam* LXVII? Refer to details in the poem in your answer.

9 (a) Look again at *The Lotos-Eaters* and write about Tennyson's narrative methods.
   (b) How far would you agree with the view that in *The Lotos-Eaters* and *Choric Song* the mariners fail in their attempt to persuade Ulysses – and us – that drug addiction is an attractive way of life?

10 Explore the ways in which Tennyson conveys a sense of hope and excitement in *In Memoriam* CVI. Refer to details in the poem in your answer.

11 How does Tennyson present thoughts and feelings about dying in *Crossing the Bar*? Refer to details in the poem in your answer.

12 Some critics have described Tennyson's poetry as 'morbid'. To what extent do you feel that Tennyson's poetry shows a gloomy preoccupation with 'unwholesome' subjects such as death, madness and despair? In your answer you should **either** refer to **two** or **three** poems in detail **or** range more widely through the whole selection.

13 What do you find memorable about the ways Tennyson portrays the experience of madness in *Maud* Part II no. V? Refer to details in the poem in your answer.

14 (a) How does Tennyson tell the story in Part IV of *The Lady of Shalott*?
   (b) To what extent do you agree with the view that women are always presented as weak, helpless victims in Tennyson's poetry?

15 Read this poem from *In Memoriam*, then look back at *In Memoriam* VII.
   CXIX
   Doors, where my heart was used to beat
       So quickly, not as one that weeps
       I come once more; the city sleeps;
   I smell the meadow in the street;

I hear a chirp of birds; I see
    Betwixt the black fronts long-withdrawn
    A light-blue lane of early dawn,
And think of early days and thee,

And bless thee, for thy lips are bland,
    And bright the friendship of thine eye;
    And in my thoughts with scarce a sigh
I take the pressure of thine hand.

Write a detailed comparison of how these two poems present the environment and the feelings of the poet.

16 Remind yourself of *'Tears, idle tears'* (from *The Princess*). To what extent do you agree with the view that this poem holds the key to the whole selection?

17 Tennyson once said that he thought he was the greatest master of the English language since Shakespeare, but that he 'had nothing to say'. How far would you agree with his assessment of himself?

18 Remind yourself of *In Memoriam* L. How far would you agree that this would form an effective conclusion to the whole selection?

19 (a) Write about the ways Tennyson tells the story in *Tithonus*.
(b) How far would you agree with the view that Tennyson avoided endings in his poems?

Chronology

Tennyson's life

1809	Born in Lincolnshire, fourth child (of 12) of George Tennyson, rector of Somersby, and Elizabeth Fytche.
1815	Attends Louth Grammar School.
1820	Leaves school to be educated at home.
1824	Father suffers mental and physical breakdown.
1827	*Poems by Two Brothers* published. Enters Trinity College, Cambridge.
1829	Begins friendship with Arthur Hallam. Joins 'Cambridge Apostles' and wins Chancellor's gold medal for poetry.
1830	*Poems, Chiefly Lyrical* published. Visit to the Pyrenees with Hallam.
1832	*Poems* published. Travels in Germany with Hallam.
1833	Hallam becomes engaged to his sister Emily Tennyson. Hallam dies (September).
1834	Tennyson falls in love with Rosa Baring.
1837	Family moves to Epping, Essex.
1838	Becomes engaged to Emily Sellwood. *Locksley Hall* completed.
1840	Breaks off engagement to Emily. Family moves to Tunbridge Wells, Kent.
1842	*Poems* enlarged version published.

1843	Loses his fortune through bad investment.
1844	Emotional breakdown.
1845	Receives Civil List pension of £200 per year.
1847	*The Princess* published.
1849	Renews correspondence with Emily.
1850	*In Memoriam* published anonymously. Marries Emily. Appointed Poet Laureate.
1851	Travels in Italy with Emily.
1852	Son Hallam is born. *Ode on the Death of the Duke of Wellington* published.
1853	Moves to Farringford on the Isle of Wight.
1854	Son Lionel is born. *The Charge of the Light Brigade* published.
1855	*Maud and Other Poems* published.
1859	First four *Idylls of the King* published.
1862	*Idylls of the King* dedicated to Prince Albert. Audience with Queen Victoria.
1864	*Enoch Arden and Other Poems* published.
1869	*The Holy Grail and Other Poems* published.
1872	*Gareth and Lynette* published.
1876	*Queen Mary* (play) produced at the Lyceum theatre and *Harold* (play) published.
1879	Death of his brother Charles. *The Falcon* (play) produced. *Ballads and Other Poems* published.
1881	*The Cup* (play) produced by Henry Irving.
1882	*The Promise of May* (play) produced.

1883   Queen Victoria makes Tennyson a baronet.

1884   Continues writing plays.

1885   *Balin and Balan* and *Tiresias and Other Poems*
        published.

1886   Son Lionel dies. *Locksley Hall Sixty Years After*
        published.

1888   Suffers serious illness, but recovers.

1889   *Demeter and Other Poems* published.

1890   Thomas Edison records Tennyson reading *The Charge
        of the Light Brigade*.

1892   Dies 6 October. Buried in Westminster Abbey.

Historical, literary and cultural events

1812   The French, under Napoleon, invade Russia but
        are forced to retreat. Lord Byron: *Childe Harold's
        Pilgrimage*. Robert Browning born.

1814   Napoleon banished to Elba. Jane Austen: *Mansfield
        Park*.

1815   Napoleon defeated at Battle of Waterloo. Corn Laws
        passed. William Wordsworth: *Poems*.

1819   Birth of Queen Victoria. 'Peterloo' massacre in
        Manchester. John Keats: *Hyperion*.

1820   Death of George III; succeeded by the Prince Regent,
        George IV. P.B. Shelley: *Prometheus Unbound*. Keats:
        Poems.

1821   Death of Keats. Shelley: *Adonais*.

1822   Death of Shelley.

1824	Death of Byron.
1825	First passenger railway opens between Stockton and Darlington. William Hazlitt: *The Spirit of the Age*.
1828	Duke of Wellington becomes prime minister.
1830	George IV dies; succeeded by William IV. Revolution in France. Charles Lyell: *Principles of Geology*.
1832	First Reform Act modernizes the electoral system.
1833	Robert Browning: *Pauline*. Abolition of slavery in the British Empire.
1834	New Poor Law passed. Burning of Houses of Parliament. The Tolpuddle Martyrs sentenced to transportation to Australia.
1837	Death of William IV; Victoria becomes queen.
1838	Formation of Anti-Corn Law League. Chartist Movement begins. Charles Darwin: *The Voyage of the Beagle*.
1840	Marriage of Victoria and Albert.
1842	Chartist petition and riots. Browning: *Dramatic Lyrics*.
1843	Thomas Carlyle: *Past and Present*. Charles Dickens: *A Christmas Carol*.
1844	Elizabeth Barrett Browning: *Poems*.
1845	Benjamin Disraeli: *Sybil*. Browning: *Dramatic Romances and Lyrics*.
1846	Repeal of Corn Laws. Famine in Ireland.
1847	Factory Act restricts working day for women and children to 10 hours. W.M. Thackeray: *Vanity Fair*. Charlotte Brontë: *Jane Eyre*. Emily Brontë: *Wuthering Heights*.

1848 Gold rush in California. Revolutions in Europe. Napoleon III elected in France. Karl Marx: *The Communist Manifesto*. Dickens: *Dombey and Son*.

1849 Dickens: *David Copperfield*.

1850 Death of Wordsworth. Barrett Browning: *Sonnets from the Portuguese*.

1851 The Great Exhibition.

1852 Dickens: *Bleak House*.

1853 Matthew Arnold: *Poems*. Charlotte Brontë: *Villette*. Elizabeth Gaskell: *Ruth* and *Cranford*.

1854 Outbreak of Crimean War; battles at Alma, Balaclava and Inkerman.

1855 Browning: *Men and Women*. Dickens: *Little Dorrit*.

1856 Crimean War ends; British war with China begins.

1857 Indian Mutiny. Barrett Browning: *Aurora Leigh*.

1859 Charles Darwin: *On the Origin of Species*.

1861 Death of Prince Albert. American Civil War begins.

1862 George Meredith: *Modern Love*.

1864 Establishment of Geneva Convention. Louis Pasteur invents pasteurization process. Dickens: *Our Mutual Friend*.

1865 American Civil War ends. Assassination of Abraham Lincoln. Lewis Carroll: *Alice in Wonderland*.

1867 Second Reform Act gives the vote to some working-class men. Invention of dynamite.

1868 William Ewart Gladstone becomes prime minister. Browning: *The Ring and the Book*.

1869	Arnold: *Culture and Anarchy*. John Stuart Mill: 'The Subjection of Women'.
1870	Franco-Prussian War. Education Act provides for educating children to the age of 12. Death of Dickens.
1871	George Eliot: *Middlemarch*. Legalization of trade unions.
1872	Civil war in Spain.
1874	Disraeli becomes prime minister. Thomas Hardy: *Far From the Madding Crowd*.
1875	Britain gains control of Suez Canal. Public Health Act.
1876	Victoria becomes Empress of India. Alexander Graham Bell invents the telephone.
1879	Anglo-Zulu War. Thomas Edison produces first electric light bulb.
1880	Gladstone prime minister again.
1881	End of First Boer War.
1883	Robert Louis Stevenson: *Treasure Island*.
1884	Third Reform Act extends voting rights to more men.
1885	Building of the first internal combustion engine to run a car. Discovery of radio waves.
1886	Hardy: *The Mayor of Casterbridge*.
1887	Queen Victoria's golden jubilee.
1888	Jack the Ripper murders several women in London.
1889	W.B. Yeats: *Crossways*.
1890	Oscar Wilde: *The Picture of Dorian Gray*. Underground railway opens in London.
1891	Hardy: *Tess of the d'Urbervilles*.

Further Reading

Editions of Tennyson's poems

The standard edition is:
Christopher Ricks (ed.), *The Poems of Tennyson* (Longman, 1969)

Editions of selected poems available in paperback include:
Michael Baron (ed.), *Alfred, Lord Tennyson* (Everyman, 1996)
Christopher Ricks (ed.), *Alfred, Lord Tennyson: Selected Poems* (Penguin Classics, 2007)
Adam Roberts (ed.), *Alfred Tennyson: The Major Works* (Oxford World's Classics, 2000)

Biography and criticism

John D. Jump (ed.), *Tennyson: The Critical Heritage* (Routledge, 1967) – an illuminating collection of nineteenth-century reviews
Robert Bernard Martin, *Tennyson: The Unquiet Heart* (Faber, 1980) – an enormous, but fascinating, account of his life and work
Christopher Ricks, *Tennyson* (Macmillan, Masters of World Literature Series, 1972)
Hallam Tennyson, *Alfred, Lord Tennyson: A Memoir by his Son*, 2 volumes (Macmillan, 1897, reprinted by Cambridge University Press, 2012) – the standard biography by his son
Aaron Watson, *Tennyson: A Biography* (T.C. & E.C. Jack, 1901, reprinted by Forgotten Books, Classic Reprint Series, 2012) – an approachable short biography; a little dated, but lively

Background reading

Joseph Bristow (ed.), *The Cambridge Companion to Victorian Poetry* (Cambridge University Press, 2000)

Steven Croft (ed.), *Victorian Literature* (Oxford University Press, Oxford Student Texts Series, 2009)

Philip Davis, *The Victorians – Oxford English Literary History, Volume 8: 1830–1880* (Oxford University Press, 2002)

Philip Davis, *Why Victorian Literature Still Matters* (Wiley, 2008)

A.N. Wilson, *The Victorians* (Hutchinson, 2002)

Other media

The Victorian Web: http://www.victorianweb.org

BBC Radio 4 Podcast (available to download) *In Our Time* Thursday 10 January 2008, 21.30, Tennyson's *The Charge of the Light Brigade*: Melvin Bragg and his guests discuss the poem http://www.bbc.co.uk/programmes/b008md8x

BBC Radio 4 Podcast (available to download) *In Our Time* Thursday 30 June 2011, 21.30, Tennyson's *In Memoriam*: Melvin Bragg and his guests discuss Tennyson's long poem http://www.bbc.co.uk/programmes/b0124pnq

Tennyson reads *The Charge of the Light Brigade*, recorded by Thomas Edison in 1890 http://www.bbc.co.uk/arts/poetry/outloud/tennyson.shtml